Building the High-Trust Organization

A Joint Publication of

The Jossey-Bass

Business & Management Series

and

The International Association

of Business Communicators

Building the High-Trust Organization

Strategies for Supporting Five Key Dimensions of Trust

Pamela S. Shockley-Zalabak,
Sherwyn P. Morreale, and
Michael Z. Hackman

IABC INTERNATIONAL ASSOCIATION
OF BUSINESS COMMUNICATORS

JB JOSSEY-BASS
A Wiley Imprint
www.josseybass.com

Published by Jossey-Bass
A Wiley Imprint
989 Market Street, San Francisco, CA 94103-1741—www.josseybass.com

Readers should be aware that Internet Web sites offered as citations and/or sources for further information may have changed or disappeared between the time this was written and when it is read.

Limit of Liability/Disclaimer of Warranty: While the publisher and author have used their best efforts in preparing this book, they make no representations or warranties with respect to the accuracy or completeness of the contents of this book and specifically disclaim any implied warranties of merchantability or fitness for a particular purpose. No warranty may be created or extended by sales representatives or written sales materials. The advice and strategies contained herein may not be suitable for your situation. You should consult with a professional where appropriate. Neither the publisher nor author shall be liable for any loss of profit or any other commercial damages, including but not limited to special, incidental, consequential, or other damages.

Jossey-Bass books and products are available through most bookstores. To contact Jossey-Bass directly call our Customer Care Department within the U.S. at 800-956-7739, outside the U.S. at 317-572-3986, or fax 317-572-4002.

Jossey-Bass also publishes its books in a variety of electronic formats. Some content that appears in print may not be available in electronic books.

Library of Congress Cataloging-in-Publication Data
Shockley-Zalabak, Pamela.
   Building the high-trust organization: strategies for supporting five key dimensions of trust / Pamela Shockley-Zalabak, Sherwyn Morreale, and Michael Z. Hackman.—1st ed.
      p.   cm.
   Includes bibliographical references and index.
   ISBN 978-0-470-39472-4 (cloth/cd-rom)
      1. Organizational behavior.   2. Trust.   3. Corporate culture—Moral and ethical aspects.
4. Organizational effectiveness.   I. Morreale, Sherwyn P.   II. Hackman, Michael Z.
III. Title.
   HD58.7.S552 2010
   658.3'14—dc22

                                                                    2009043623

Printed in the United States of America

FIRST EDITION

HB Printing   10 9 8 7 6 5 4 3 2 1
PB Printing   10 9 8 7 6 5 4 3 2 1

Contents

Contents of the CD

The Organizational Trust Index (OTI)

Analyzing Your Organization's Results from the Organizational Trust Index

Form 1: Analyzing Organizational Results, Areas of Strength

Form 2: Analyzing Organizational Results, Areas of Improvement

Form 3: Analyzing Organizational Results, Areas of Strength for Reinforcement

Form 4: Analyzing Organizational Results, Areas for Improvement

Scoring Instrument for the Organization Trust Index

A Facilitation Approach for Comprehensive Improvement of Organizational Trust

Sample Educational Outlines for Building High Trust Organizations

To our clients, colleagues, and students.
Thank you for placing your trust in us.

Preface

We first became interested in organizational trust more than a decade ago. At that time we were convinced trust played a significant role in impacting overall organizational effectiveness. Our subsequent research conducted in several countries around the world, consulting experiences on four continents, and observations of the widespread "trust crash" that occurred over the past couple of years have only served to convince us trust is not just critically important—*it is the main thing*—the essential element of organizational success. We hope after reading this book you also will be convinced building trust is critical to your success and the overall success of your organization.

High-trust organizations have increased value, accelerated growth, enhanced innovation, improved collaboration, stronger partnering, better execution, and heightened loyalty. A 2002 study showed high-trust organizations outperformed low-trust organizations by 286 percent in total return to shareholders (stock price plus dividends.) A 2005 study supported these findings suggesting high-trust organizations earned more than four times the returns of the broader market over the prior seven years.[1] Recent examples, several of which are discussed in this book, ranging from Enron to Bear Stearns, Lehman Brothers, and AIG, support the notion that, without trust, organizations cannot thrive.

This book is divided into three parts. In Part One, we address some of the common misconceptions about trust and introduce our organizational trust model. The model and the Organizational Trust Index (OTI) have been demonstrated to be stable across different cultures and industries. The twenty-nine-question OTI, which is included on a CD at the back of this book, was validated by surveying over four thousand employees in a wide range of business sectors in eight different countries around the world. The organizational trust model and the OTI are based on five key drivers of organizational trust: *competence, openness and honesty, concern for employees/stakeholders, reliability, and identification*.

Each of these organizational trust drivers is discussed in detail in Part Two of the book. To explore these trust dimensions in depth, we include detailed strategies for building each driver of trust in your organization. We also provide a Trust in Action case summary at the end of each chapter in Part Two. Our cases demonstrate how each trust driver has been applied effectively within a well-known organization. Finally, we provide a list of ten Trust Lessons as takeaways from each chapter.

In Part Three of the book, we discuss how to create and build trust in your organization. We look at some of the significant trust challenges faced by many organizations: globalization; the virtual world of work; innovation, creativity and risk; and conflict and crisis. In the last chapter of the book and in the Appendix, we discuss comprehensive steps that can be taken to build organizational trust.

We have reviewed more than 3,500 articles in the research literature on trust and have worked with hundreds of organizations on issues related to improving communication and leadership effectiveness. We have interviewed and talked with leaders in organizations in over twenty-five countries, including the United States, Asia, Africa, Europe, Australia, and the Mid-East. Our conclusion is clear: *trust is the main thing in any organization*. More importantly, organizational trust can be improved. We hope this book helps to start you on your journey to gain a better understanding of the importance of trust and the value of building trust in your organization. We have provided a number of tools you can use to support trust building in your organization. These tools will serve as a good beginning point in becoming a high-trust organization. We are available to assist in your journey should you feel you need guidance in developing a more comprehensive strategy. We wish all who read this book success in building high-trust organizations that demonstrate competence, openness and honesty, concern for employees/stakeholders, reliability, and identification.

Pamela Shockley-Zalabak
  pshockle@uccs.edu
Sherwyn Morreale
  smorreal@uccs.edu
Michael Z. Hackman
  mhackman@uccs.edu
Colorado Springs, Colorado
January 2010

Part One

INTRODUCING THE TRUST MODEL

"This world of ours . . . must avoid becoming a community of dreadful fear and hate, and be, instead, a proud confederation of mutual trust and respect."

—*Dwight D. Eisenhower, thirty-fourth President of the United States, 1890–1969*

In Part One, we argue strongly that trust in organizations is not just critically important—it is the *main thing*—the essential element of organizational success. We first introduce you to several common myths about the nature of trust, with an emphasis on the high cost to organizations of distrust and betrayal. We describe organizational trust and then talk about why it is so important. We next consider the intimate relationship of trust to achieving organizational excellence. Perhaps most important, we introduce you to our research-based model of organizational trust and its five no-nonsense components: competence, openness, concern, reliability, and identification.

1

ORGANIZATIONAL TRUST

What Does It Mean? Why Does It Matter?

"Trust men [and women] and they will be true
to you; treat them greatly and they will show
themselves great."

—*Ralph Waldo Emerson, American*
author and poet, 1803–1882

When one of our long-term clients asked us to go to Seattle to meet with the leaders of their newest division, we frankly were surprised. The formation of the new division had been part of a massive strategic planning effort to locate research and develop capacity for the company's medical products line near other important company operations. The division leaders and engineering personnel had been hand-picked from highly successful development teams throughout the company. The fact that several key personnel were asking to return to their previous assignments did not make sense. We met first with division manager, Larry Reynolds, who was highly regarded for leading several product introductions resulting in record-breaking sales.[1] Larry was baffled and somewhat angry about the vocal resistance to the direction he was trying to take the division. After we talked with the engineers who had publicly stated they wanted to leave, the issue became clear. The engineers did not trust Larry knew what he was doing. They trusted Larry as an individual but not his expertise to develop the new product lines. They agreed he had been extremely successful with past product introductions but believed they knew more about the future direction medical products should take. They claimed he would not listen to alternative approaches or attempt to agree on a common vision. They did not want to risk their careers in this new venture and were trying to find a way to get corporate management to listen. They had succeeded.

Our experience with Larry Reynolds and his engineers focused our thinking around the importance of trust and the need to help our clients understand trust building as fundamental to their success. Larry Reynolds was on the verge of failing, and he didn't like it one bit. And Larry was no different from countless other people with whom we had worked. Most books don't start with the notion of failure. But that is where we are going to start. Unfortunately, Larry Reynolds and his engineers are not unusual examples of what happens when trust begins to break down. Larry's experience happens daily in hundreds, even thousands, of organizations. As a result, we believe if you read only one leadership, management, communication, or business book this year, it should be this one. We know from our experience that many people are like Larry. While they in fact can be trusted, they are not naturally trust-builders. The trust-building model we present in this book is practical and research tested in over sixty organizations throughout the world. Some say the model is common sense, but we know it is uncommon practice.

Wayne Hutchens, president of the University of Colorado Foundation, has a saying that fits what we know about trust in organizational life. Hutchens, in talking about the importance of focus, says, "The main thing is always the main thing." As you read this book, we hope to convince you the *main thing* is trust and this main thing is fundamental to building and maintaining successful organizations. So, yes, in this chapter we begin with failure—distrust and betrayal—and its costs. We describe common myths about trust, when believed, contribute to distrust in organizations. We talk about the concept of organizational trust and why it is the *"main thing"* for organizational excellence.

Finally, we explore how we begin to develop trust traditions and how we make decisions to trust.

The High Cost of Distrust

"Trust dies but mistrust blossoms."
—*Sophocles, Greek playwright, 496–406 B.C.*

The engineers' distrust of Larry Reynolds' competence when it came to introducing new medical products was close to derailing the overall success of the division. The company was about to pay a high price for not recognizing the negative ramifications of distrust and why it occurs. Unfortunately, often this type of distrust is easier than trust in many relationships. There are no surprises, no need to feel vulnerable, and no disappointments. I may feel disgust when you break your word, but I won't feel betrayed because I expected you to fail me. Distrusting relationships are characterized by low interdependence; I simply won't depend on you because I don't think I can and I don't want you depending on me. I don't listen to your ideas because I don't expect them to be worth it. I don't expect you to produce anything of special worth, and I would not believe it if you did. Chances are we will never work together very effectively.

The global financial crisis that began in 2008 produced a history-making example of distrust, a situation we describe as a sweeping and almost unprecedented "trust crash." The bond between creditor and borrower is built on trust and believing in one another. Indeed, the word credit originates with the Latin term, *credo*, meaning belief.[2] Few would disagree distrust has replaced trust for many if not the majority of financial institutions. One banker with whom we work summed it up, "I never thought I would have to tell customers we are local, not tied in with the big guys; we are not taking any federal bailout money, and we aren't giving bonuses to our executives. Just months ago, being small and local was a disadvantage. The distrust has fractured relationships for years to come. Now people distrust us for no reason. We have to work hard to get them to trust us just because of what others have done." Distrust can have the following high costs for any organization.

Distrust Contributes to "We Versus Them" Behavior

"I know my work group is producing, but others aren't. We won't share how we solved the problem because we will look better if we win. You can't trust others to give credit where it is due. It is hard enough to trust those immediately around me, so don't ask me to trust people I don't know."

Over the years we have worked with IT departments in many companies. In several instances we have observed a "we versus them" conflict between IT development and operations groups. Developers are responsible for creating the technical architecture required to build websites, databases, and other IT systems. Those in operations support these systems so that customers can use what has been built by developers. This delineation of roles makes sense. Developers spend their time creating new systems, and those in operations provide support for these systems to internal and external customers. Yet, in practice, there are often significant issues of distrust between these two groups. Often this is the result of how performance is measured. Developers are most often rewarded for meeting deadlines, while those in operations are evaluated based on reducing system down-time. Developers have frequently reported to us they don't give operations people all of the information about a system because they don't believe they have the expertise to understand the nuances. When a system has bugs or, worse yet, crashes, it is a top priority for operations to find a solution. They frequently distrust developers whom they believe did not give them adequate system information and are not motivated to help because of the need to abandon new projects in an effort to solve problems for something already in use. This is a classic example of a "we versus them" approach leading to distrust.

Distrust Lowers Employee Desire to Contribute to Productivity Goals

Employees have expectations when they join an employer, often unwritten but important perceptions about what they can expect. Beliefs about job security, benefits, and concern for employee welfare, communication, and treatment from management all contribute to trust expectations between employees and employers. When employees believe their employer is either overtly or marginally "breaking" the expectations, many, if not most, employees cease to make extra efforts to produce. Downsizing is a perfect example of an organizational action strongly impacting trust and "breaking" expectations. The data suggest downsizing often leaves behind a workforce that is demoralized, angry, and discouraged. More important for the long-term viability of the organization—survivors often are cautious, unwilling to make decisions or take risks, and lacking in energy and commitment. A study by the American Management Association found 40 percent of organizations reported productivity had fallen after downsizing, and 18 percent reported quality had suffered. Morale was hit even harder: 58 percent said morale had decreased, and 37 percent of organizations reported employees were more difficult to retain.[3] When employees no longer trust their employers, even rewards such as pay raises or promotions will not easily restore trust.[4]

Distrust Breeds Fear and Destructive Behaviors

When managers fear what is going to happen from top leaders, when employees fear their supervisors, when competitor performance generates fear, or when the unknown simply paralyzes decision making, bad things happen. Individuals differ greatly in their responses to fear. Some attempt to get even or engage in revenge, while others retreat from the situation and avoid solving problems. Hidden agendas, dishonesty, gossip, conflict, and denial flourish. The organization loses opportunities to solve problems.

We return to the global financial crisis as an example of unprecedented fear generating destructive behaviors. We confirmed our understanding of the crisis by talking with U.S. and international experts to help us understand the underpinnings of the fear associated with the financial crisis. We first talked with Jim Paulsen, chief investment strategist for Wells Capital Management, when he came to Colorado Springs for the Southern Colorado Economic Forum.[5] Since 1983, Paulsen has been a frequent national commentator on a wide range of financial issues. Paulsen said to us and others attending the forum, "Fear itself, more than fundamental problems, is causing the crisis. Fear comes from the absence of trust. . . . We are running people out of business by fear." He went on to assert, in his opinion, not one of the financial markets in 2008 was trading on fundamentals but they were, instead, trading on emotion and fear. Paulsen described the need for U.S. political leadership to sell the $700 billion relief package (TARP) to the public. To do that, leaders were forced to say the country was financially going under if the package did not pass the U.S. House and Senate. The President and Congressional leaders had to generate yet more fear in order to pass the package, resulting in the worst confidence crisis since the depression and the perception that we as a nation were without competent leaders. Paulson's remarks reminded us of Barry Glassner's description of U.S. society in the 21st century as becoming a "culture of fear."[6]

Paulsen was not the only one making this argument. On October 1, 2008, *New York Times* columnist and best-selling author, Thomas Friedman, wrote about being frightened for his country only a few times in his life:

"In 1962, when, even as a boy of nine, I followed the tension of the Cuban missile crisis; in 1963, with the assassination of

J.F.K.; on September 11, 2001; and on Monday, when the House Republicans brought down the bipartisan rescue package. But this moment is the scariest of all for me because the previous three were all driven by real or potential attacks on the U.S. system by outsiders. This time, we are doing it to ourselves. . . . I've always believed that America's government was a unique political system— one designed by geniuses so that it could be run by idiots. I was wrong. No system can be smart enough to survive this level of incompetence and recklessness by the people charged to run it. . . . This is a credit crisis. It's all about confidence."[7]

In late October 2008, we traveled to Granada, Spain, for the global SIETAR Congress. Discussions of the financial crisis were front and center. Nigel Ewington, founding director of both TEC International Diversity Management and WorldWork Ltd., predicted a "downward spiral of trust in business leadership because of the present global situation."[8] Another WorldWork, Ltd. director, Richard Lowe, was even more specific. Lowe claimed, "The current global financial crisis is destroying trust. Rebuilding trust will become a major priority."[9] He went on to contend, and we agree, there will be less transparency during the downturn as senior managers keep to themselves when planning for an uncertain future. A Weber Shandwick/KRC Research survey released in November 2008 in *USA Today* supported our concerns. When asked whether company leaders communicated with employees about how the current economy might affect their organization, 70 percent said no, 1 percent did not know, and only 29 percent responded yes.[10]

During the fall, 2008 U.S. election season, one of us received a direct mail piece that summed up the trust crisis, "You know you can't trust these guys—Wall Street, Lehman Brothers, AIG."[11] For us, Sasha Abramsky, a journalist and lecturer at the University of California–Davis best describes what can happen when fear replaces trust: "In a world of panic responses, economic downturns can all too easily morph into full-scale calamities."[12]

Distrust Makes Crises Worse

Trust is difficult to regain once lost, and a crisis provides no time for repair. The examples from the financial crisis are multiple. However, they are by no means unique. When a chief executive officer attempts to explain a major product failure or a poor financial performance, distrust among customers or shareholders causes suspicion to rise. People are more likely to pursue litigation following a crisis when they distrust what they have been told or experienced. This is particularly true in the physician-patient relationship. A number of studies note that poor communication and a lack of trust are more likely to lead to malpractice litigation than a doctor's performance—even when something has clearly gone wrong and it is the physician's fault. In one study of malpractice depositions, communication and trust breakdowns between the physician and the patient were noted in 70 percent of the cases. Doctors with no malpractice claims against them used a variety of trust-building strategies, including checking for patient understanding, educating patients about what to expect during their visits, and encouraging patients to talk.[13] Clearly distrust in the physician-patient relationship was a significant factor in escalating a medical error into a malpractice suit.

Distrust Is Expensive

Most would agree the U.S. Sarbanes-Oxley Act with its myriad of financial compliance obligations costs money and is fundamentally related to breaches of trust.[14] Monitoring and surveillance systems, highly prescriptive contracts, extensive rules and regulations, low supervisor to employee ratios, and a host of other organizational processes require substantial resources both human and financial. In one way or another, these business decisions or processes are reflective of distrust.

We are not arguing that distrust always is wrong, but that it is fundamentally more expensive than trust. And we believe distrust is present, at least in part, because of our tendency to buy into an array of myths about the nature of trust.

Myths About Trust

All of us have assumptions about trust. Some of us trust almost everyone. Others trust few. The pitfalls of our assumptions usually become obvious only after unpleasant experiences. We suffer a breach of trust. We at first don't trust someone who turns out to be a star performer and, in turn, that person distrusts us because of our initial discounting. Most of us don't think consciously about building trust or distrust as a part of our daily activities. But our own false assumptions and collective myths about trust unconsciously affect all that we do in organizations. The following trust myths illustrate our point.

A widespread belief suggests that *trust matters but there is little we can do about it*. This book will challenge that myth by providing concrete ways for individuals and entire organizations to become trust-builders. You will learn from the successes and failures of leaders, and you will see what successful organizations have done to increase their trust profiles.

Many individuals know themselves to be trustworthy and expect others to trust them based on their own personal evaluations. The myth, simply put, is, *if I am trustworthy, others will trust me*. Our client, Larry Reynolds, was making that mistake with a group of skeptical and disagreeing engineers. They knew Larry was personally trustworthy but had real concerns about his competence in their new area of work. The trust gap was huge. Larry was making the mistake of thinking that, because his intentions were good, no one could misinterpret his behaviors.

It is hard to face the myth that *integrity does not equate to trust*. Integrity is fundamental for trust, but organizational trust requires a more sophisticated alignment among intentions, behaviors, and interpretations of behaviors. Organizational trust is a gestalt of organizational intentions and behaviors and the interpretations of those intentions and behaviors. This alignment is neither simple nor common practice. There are often significant differences between intentions and how behaviors are interpreted. We refer to this difference as the *trust gap*. Organizational trust results from intentions, behaviors, and interpretations and, equally important, influences intentions, behaviors, and interpretations. The trust model we will present helps both individuals and organizations bridge the intentions-behavior-interpretation trust gap.

Describing Trust

"In the 1960s, if you introduced a new product to America, 90 percent of the people who viewed it for the first time believed in the corporate promise. Then forty years later if you performed the same exercise, less than 10 percent of the public believed it was true. The fracturing of trust is based on the fact that the consumer has been let down."

—*Howard Schultz, owner and current CEO of Starbucks*

So what is this "*main thing*" we are calling organizational trust? Definitions are numerous and they vary. Based on our experience and the research-based model presented in this book, we describe organizational trust as *the overarching belief that an organization in its communication and behaviors is competent, open and honest, concerned, reliable, and worthy of identification with its goals, norms, and values*. The following descriptors further clarify this definition.

Trust Is a Multifaceted Experience in Organizations

Most of us would agree with this concept. If we think about it, we recognize that we experience self-trust and distrust. We have many types of individual relationships within the organization, ranging from peers to managers to top leaders. We work in groups and with networks of people we may or may not meet face-to-face. We work between organizations and with customers, vendors, and a variety of other stakeholders. We work within a broad societal framework that is growing more important all of the time with increases in global connections. All of these relationships are influenced in one way or another by trust.

Some of our trust evaluations come from direct knowledge and personal interactions. Others are drawn from knowledge that is indirect, impersonal, and based on affiliations or reputations. For example, when strangers from two different organizations engage in a business transaction and discover they both came from the same business school and have shared the same professors, they may be more likely to trust based on the generalized knowledge of shared norms, values, and behaviors from their educational institution. However, if one of the individuals had a bad experience with the school in question and the other a good experience, the contradictory perceptions may contribute to distrust.

Trust Is Culturally Determined

Because of this concept, universal laws regarding organizational trust are elusive. Much has been made over the last several years about the importance of organizational cultures. It is important, therefore, to realize that the context for organizational life is embedded within national and regional cultures. Organizational trust therefore is specific to the organization's culture but also to the dominant society and culture of which the organization is a part. We have worked as consultants in organizations all around the globe. During our travels we have discovered that trust-building behaviors are culturally dependent. Actions that enhance trust in one culture may have only a negligible, or even a negative, impact in another country. In some countries in Europe, Austria, Germany, the Netherlands, and Switzerland, for example, we have discovered promptness and attention to detail are critical in building trust. Being late or being sloppy in the preparation of assignments indicates a poor work ethic and lack of professionalism. Those who do not follow these expectations may be viewed with distrust in these countries. We also have worked extensively in Italy. Here timeliness and a detail-orientation are valued by some, but have much less impact on perceptions of trust than in many other Western European countries. In Italy, as journalist Beppe Severgnini explains, "Obedience is boring. . . . [Italians] want to be treated as unique individuals."[15] Does this mean that Italians are less trustworthy than their counterparts in other part of Europe? Of course not; it simply means that the behaviors that contribute to perceptions of trust are different in Italy. Being late to a meeting may not lead an Italian executive to distrust a colleague, but an overly rigid approach, a lack of respect for culture, or poor manners may have a much more negative impact.

Trust Is Communication-Based

Perceptions of organizational trust result from acts of interpretation—in short, communication. What do employees think about the integrity of leaders during merger talks? Do stockholders believe leaders can be successful in increasingly competitive markets? How truthful is employee communication? The answers to these questions inevitably are interpretations based on experiences and perceptions of trust. It is through communication processes that individuals can describe an ideal organizational life. And it is against this ideal that they compare their current organizational experiences. When the gap is small, organizational members will report higher levels of trust, while a widening gap contributes to lower levels of trust.

Trust Is Dynamic

Trust can change rapidly based on circumstances and experiences. Trust is fluid. Anyone watching the aftermath of the failure to respond quickly to hurricane Katrina victims in New Orleans understood that agencies previously regarded as trusted to respond to emergencies came under rapid criticism, resulting in low-trust evaluations. Most claim trust is harder to rebuild once lost. However, it also is true that a long history of trust can assist when problems and crises confront either an individual or an entire organization. Just a year before the collapse of Enron, McKinsey & Company, one of the largest global management consulting firms, rated Enron (a McKinsey client generating more than $10 million in annual revenues) as one of the best success stories in business. Even after the situation at Enron became apparent, there were still nearly thirty articles on the McKinsey website with favorable comments about the company. That all changed after the collapse of Enron. Today, McKinsey executives admit their reputation was "dented" by the Enron scandal, adding that the company can't be right "every time" in evaluating organizations.[16]

Trust Is Multi-Dimensional

By this we mean trust has behavioral, cognitive, and emotional dimensions. Trust is a complex assortment of behaviors and actions (behavioral dimension), beliefs, intentions, motivations, expectations, and assumptions (cognitive dimension), and emotions and feelings (emotional dimension). Clearly, the behaviors of others impact our trust levels and whether we perceive others as trustworthy. When we catch our boss in a lie, our trust is diminished. We react at cognitive and emotional levels based on observed behaviors. Similarly, our own behaviors are interpreted cognitively and emotionally by others.

In one organization we encountered, there were two teams, each performing pretty much the same types of tasks. The team leader in one of the groups was highly interactive, walking the floor on a daily basis and having frequent conversations with her direct reports. The other team leader was much less outgoing, often holed up in his office. He gave no specific feedback to his team, leaving those who reported to him wondering what they had done "wrong" and why their manager was not willing to talk with them. Although no operational problem occurred, the reticent team leader's lack of interaction caused his direct reports to make negative cognitive and emotional assessments of their relationship. Ultimately, these negative thoughts and feelings that something was "wrong" led to distrust. By contrast, the communication behaviors (behavioral reaction) of the interactive leader resulted in positive cognitive and emotional reactions in her reports; they knew what was going on (cognitive reaction), felt good about their work and relationships (emotional reaction), and therefore trusted their leader more.

Continuums of Organizational Trust

In our description of organizational trust, we suggest that trust works on a series of continuums. The continuums we think most important are: (1) *distrust to optimal trust*; (2) *fragile to resilient trust*; and (3) *shallow to deep trust*.

Distrust to Optimal Trust Continuum

This continuum recognizes that most organizational members hold a mixture of trust and distrust in most situations, whether personal or business. And it is possible for trust to distrust swings on the continuum to be rapid and difficult to understand. Perceptions of costs, benefits, and risks in a given circumstance can move us from trust to distrust or vice versa. Part of consciously thinking about trust-building requires knowing where we individually are on the distrust to optimal trust continuum and speculating where important others are located during major decisions and change efforts.

Fragile to Resilient Trust Continuum

This continuum describes the staying power or lack thereof for trust. Resilient organizational trust happens when individuals perceive they share the same norms, values, and beliefs as their organization. In other words, they have strong organizational identification. On the other end of the continuum, fragile trust is more often experienced when individuals are uncertain how their own norms, values, and beliefs fit within the organization. Trust is hoped for, but not given without reservation.

Shallow to Deep Trust Continuum

Our final continuum relates to the amount of dependence and interdependence we have with others in the organization. If I am not dependent on you and don't need you to be successful, I may trust you, but the chances are we are on the shallow end of the continuum. I don't have or need enough interaction with you to move along to a deeper relationship of trust or distrust. If, on the other hand, I have information needs that only you can provide and my productivity is linked to yours, it is possible to say we are on the deep trust end of the continuum. I need to know where I stand with you and the reverse.

Organizations in the financial, automotive, and airline sectors exemplify the low end of the three continuums—distrust, fragility, and shallowness. As the airline companies have tried to cope with first increasing fuel costs and then a slowing economy, their responses to changing economic conditions have resulted in high levels of distrust on the part of employees and customers. As a case in point, pilots and their unions at two major airlines, American and US Airways, have complained privately and publicly the airlines were forcing pilots to fly uncomfortably low on fuel in order to cut costs. Pilots, flight dispatchers, and others claimed safety for passengers was compromised, while the Federal Aviation Administration said there was no reason to order airlines to back off their effort to keep fuel loads to a minimum as a cost-saving strategy.[17] US Airways pilots took out a full-page ad in *USA Today* to alert the flying public to this danger. Needless to say, airline pilots, other employees, and the public came to distrust the airline executives making and implementing the fuel load decision.

The 2008 meltdown in the financial sector produced a widespread trust crisis that significantly damaged perceptions of trust in a broad range of financial institutions from local banks to global investment firms. Trust in these organizations became so fragile that customers withdrew billions of dollars in deposits and investments from financial institutions such as Bear Stearns, IndyMac Bank, and Washington Mutual, believing their money would be safer if it were not held by these institutions.[18] This far-reaching bank run only uncovered more violations of trust such as Bernie Madoff's more than $65-billion hedge fund fraud, further shattering confidence among consumers.

Trust in the automobile industry has recently been characterized by shallowness. When the U.S. government first proposed a bailout plan in 2008 to provide financial assistance to the big three U.S. automobile manufacturers—GM, Ford, and Chrysler— a Gallup poll indicated almost half (49 percent) of Americans were opposed to the plan. In response to a later question regarding the bailout, only a slight majority (56 percent) supported providing government assistance, even if one of the big three was **certain to fail** without such assistance.[19] Seemingly 44 percent of those surveyed had such shallow trust in the U.S. automobile industry that they would be willing to allow a U.S. automobile manufacturer to cease production before they would be willing to invest American tax dollars to keep the company operating.

By contrast to the trust erosion in the airline industry, financial institutions, and automobile manufacturers, the retailer Costco is a good example of an organization on the high end of the optimal, resilient, and deep trust continuums. Jim Sinegal, co-founder and the long-time CEO at Costco, began his career at age eighteen unloading mattresses in a month-old venture called Fed-Mart. After several acquisitions and start-ups, Fed-Mart morphed into Costco in the early 1980s. Today Costco is the fourth-largest retailer in the United States with some five hundred stores in thirty-seven states and eight countries and sales exceeding $50 billion a year. Costco is a warehouse merchandiser in the mold of Sam's Club or Wal-Mart and sells everything from wine (more than any other single retailer in the world) and salmon fillets to flat-screen TVs and leather sofas. But while Sam's Club and Wal-Mart have been criticized for being driven strictly by profit, Costco has adopted a values-driven approach that has resulted in moving them to the high end of the trust continuums.[20]

Costco's resilient trust is explained in part by employees' identification with a company that values their contributions. CEO Sinegal believes employees should be paid fair wages for their valuable contributions to the organization. In 2006, the average Costco warehouse employee earned $17 per hour—40 percent more than the amount paid by other warehouse merchandisers. Costco also offered better-than-average benefits, including health care coverage, to more than 90 percent of its workforce. As Sinegal explained, there is a real business advantage in treating employees well. He calls his 120,000 loyal employees "ambassadors." These employees trust Costco and believe in its values. Because of this, Costco has the lowest employee turnover rate in retailing.[21]

Costco not only encourages interdependence among employees, but the company extends that value to customers and external stakeholders. Costco, for instance, has a trade-in and recycle program in which customers can turn in old electronic devices to be recycled when they purchase new ones. As a result, various stakeholders, including workers, report deep trust in Costco.[22]

The Pyramid of Trust in Figure 1.1 illustrates how these three continuums converge to produce high trust. Conversely, when they diverge, trust is low.

Many of the descriptions of trust we have just provided can apply to either individuals or entire organizations. And in some

Figure 1.1 Pyramid of Trust

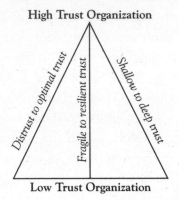

ways, the individual cannot be separated from the organization. However, the focus of this book is the organization and how individuals within the organization can consciously become trust-builders. Individual trust most often is built from personal experience. As stated earlier, organizational trust is a more complex alignment of multiple behaviors, emotions, intentions, and interpretations. Organizational trust is built from indirect and impersonal experiences. Organizational trust drives individual behaviors, which in turn become the creativity and productivity of the organization. We are convinced organizational trust is the *"main thing"* for overall effectiveness and the capacity to achieve organizational excellence.

Trust and Organizational Excellence

"The time is always right to do what is right."
—*Martin Luther King, Jr., civil rights activist and
1964 Nobel Prize winner, 1929–1968*

Shortly after we finished the research for the trust model presented in this book, we were invited to speak to a convention of personnel executives in Phoenix. We talked about the new trust model, with particular emphasis on why trust matters. The executives were amazed when we made what seemed to them strong and unsupported statements. We claimed trust is the *main thing* for organizational excellence. The evidence overwhelmingly supports our position. In sum, we were claiming trust is critical to bottom-line results, to how organizations "form" themselves, to the overall quality of work effort, and to how organizations learn.

Trust Is Fundamental for Bottom-Line Results

Numerous studies link trust and perceptions of integrity to bottom-line economic performance. Restaurants, sales forces, NCAA teams, and a host of other organizations all perform better when trust levels are high.[23] Stephen M.R. Covey has said trust is the one thing that changes everything. We agree. Covey describes the low-trust organization as requiring unnecessary duplication and bureaucracy. The low-trust organization is a political environment in which disengagement is common, turnover high, and fraud often prevalent. Covey reports high-trust organizations have increased value, accelerated growth, enhanced innovation, improved collaboration, stronger partnering, better execution, and heightened loyalty. According to Covey, "A 2002 Watson Wyatt study showed that high-trust organizations outperformed low-trust organizations by 286 percent in total return to shareholders (stock price plus dividends). A 2005 study by Russell Investment Group showed that *Fortune* magazine's '100 Best Companies to Work For'—in which trust comprises 60 percent of the criteria—earned more than four times the returns of the broader market over the prior seven years. A PricewaterhouseCoopers study of corporate innovation among the *Financial Times* 100 showed that the number one differentiating factor between the top innovators and the bottom innovators was trust."[24]

Trust Impacts Organizational Forms

Our research and work with clients supports the claim that trust impacts the ability to create adaptive organizational forms, to form strategic alliances, and to work in effective virtual teams. Why? The answer is simple. Important organizational knowledge never resides only at the top. If we cannot delegate with confidence, we must create costly redundancy and reporting structures that lower efficiency. When we can't trust, autonomous, rapid response is impossible. Problems are not solved, opportunities are missed, costs rise, and effectiveness suffers. When we can't empower diverse organizational members to work across departments to move resources rapidly in support of collaboration, any matrix created to enhance creativity fails. And when there is no trust in an organization networked with strategic partners, the organization fails.[25]

Trust Impacts Work Effort

When "a day's work for a day's pay" is tightly monitored, rarely does production exceed the expected standard. When laborers are given control over major aspects of their work, production frequently exceeds more highly supervised efforts. These findings are not new. We have ample evidence that being trusted to do a job independently creates more productive performance and change. In less observable and structured work, most agree trust has an even larger impact. The "doing an adequate but not outstanding" job is not readily measured or identified, but often is the difference between good and great organizational performance.

Trust Impacts How Organizations Learn

Creativity, innovation, and ambiguity offer major organizational opportunities. For creativity and innovation to flourish, people at all organizational levels must have the motivation to challenge conventional wisdom and push to change the status quo. Not surprisingly, creativity and innovation are likely to flourish in climates of trust and to literally shut down when distrust is prevalent. In our work as consultants, we over and over again have encountered employees who knew their organization was in trouble but did not trust their input would be welcome or would make any difference. Silence was simply the safer course of action.

Trust Is The Main Thing

In their best-selling book, *Built to Last*, Jim Collins and Jerry Porras describe what they call successful habits of visionary companies such as 3M, American Express, Boeing, Disney, Hewlett-Packard, Nordstrom, and others.[26] Our research tells us that trust is pivotal to the Collins and Porras habits. Collins and Porras describe the building of lasting organizations with core values. They describe cultures with which employees identify over a long period of time and the selection of leaders who can support core values while articulating a clear vision and sense of direction. They describe visionary and futuristic thinking, not just superb daily execution. They describe staying power during change. The model we present in the next several chapters is designed to generate the staying power that only trust can generate. Our model is designed to help leaders establish clear yet ambitious performance goals resulting in superb execution while stimulating creativity and innovation for the future.

Trust Traditions: The Decision to Trust

"The best way to find out if you can trust somebody
is to trust them."

—*Ernest Hemingway,*
1954 Nobel Prize–winning author, 1899–1961

All of us bring extensive trust traditions to our organizational lives. Family, friends, school, early organizational experiences, media, and society in general all contribute to our individual and collective trust traditions. Most of us learn somewhere along the way that trust comes with a price. The more we risk when we trust, the more vulnerable we become. The more we distrust, the fewer the surprises. We make decisions about whether to trust or not based on many factors, including our tolerance for risk and the relative power we have in a given situation. We make decisions to trust based on knowledge about others, past experiences, predictability and integrity, and the communication surrounding the person, issues, or events. We make trust decisions using direct experience and impersonal information. In major life decisions such as marriage or divorce, we may make a conscious decision about trust in a relationship. Far fewer of us recognize our daily decisions to trust or distrust, even though our trust decisions influence most of our other decisions and overall behavior. Organizational leaders make strategic decisions, changes policies and practices, and set performance goals without consciously thinking about trust implications. In the next several chapters we will describe how building trust traditions can positively influence decisions to trust. We believe the results will speak for themselves.

Chapter Lessons in Trust

1. Trust is the main thing.
2. Distrust has both human and financial costs.
3. It is a myth that we cannot do anything about trust— everything we do is about trust.
4. Trust is individual, organizational, and cultural.
5. Building trust is common sense but uncommon practice.
6. Trust is directly linked to organizational excellence.
7. Trust is linked to measurable organizational outcomes.
8. Building trust traditions pays dividends.
9. Trust-building is everyone's responsibility.
10. Your organization can become a trust builder.

2

THE ORGANIZATIONAL
TRUST MODEL

"Quality means doing it right when no one is looking."
—Henry Ford, founder of Ford Motor Company
and creator of mass production, 1863–1947

When we were presenting the organizational trust model to a group of senior executives in Vancouver, Canada, an experienced finance manager asked us a pointed question. "It all sounds good, but what makes this approach any different? Why should we believe you that your model is going to work any better than what we are doing now?" Our answer was just as direct: *"Our model has been developed based on vast amounts of previous research and experiences. The development of the model meets the highest research standards, and clients using the model have produced demonstrated results. However, we don't know whether it is any better than what you are doing now because we don't know what you are doing now."*

We learned in that brief exchange that it is not enough to convince people trust is the *main thing*. We have to establish a solid foundation for the model we are proposing. Individuals must trust the model in order to build trust in their organizations. They have a need to contrast our recommendations with what they are currently doing. The evidence needs to be compelling. We think that is fair and appropriate.

A Research-Based Model

"Responsibilities are given to him [her] on whom
trust rests. Responsibility is always a sign of trust."
—*James Cash Penney, businessman
and founder of JC Penney, 1875–1971*

The organizational trust model and the Organizational Trust Index (OTI) were originally developed by a team of researchers and practitioners supported by a research grant from the International Association of Business Communicators Research Foundation.[1] Basically, our team wanted to understand what many today find critical to their business success. So we asked: "In the face of the changing organizational landscape with its reduced interpersonal familiarity among employees scattered across the globe, how can trust contribute to an organization's ability to work effectively?" We wanted to know whether extending what we knew about organizational trust could predict job satisfaction and perceived organizational effectiveness. We wanted to collect worldwide data, in multiple languages, to determine whether the critical drivers of organizational trust were stable across cultures and industries. It was a big assignment.

To begin our work, we enlisted fifty-three organizations from Australia, Hong Kong, India, Italy, Japan, Singapore, and the United States. We were guided in our selection of organizations by both the willingness of the organizations to provide usable information and a balance among diversity of organizational types and industries; geographic dispersal of employees; and range of organizational sizes. Participating organizations had workforces between one hundred and 146,000, drawn from both manufacturing and service sectors (pharmaceuticals, chemicals, high-tech, insurance, banking, healthcare, retail, and hotels), as well as education, government, and non-profit groups. Our research began by conducting twenty cross-industry focus groups in the United States and Europe. We asked open-ended questions designed to have participants describe all of the various drivers of trust they could identify. An analysis of the focus group data reflected five emergent dimensions of organizational trust, which were then tested in a 232-item survey translated into English, Italian, Spanish, and Chinese. Over four thousand employees, randomly selected from the participating organizations, completed the survey. Respondents represented twenty-five states in the United States; eleven cities in Italy; and Sydney, Singapore, Hong Kong, Tokyo, Mumbai, and Taiwan. Validation studies reduced the survey items to the twenty-nine-question Organizational Trust Index, which is included on a CD at the back of this book.[2] The Index can be used to assess the level of trust in any organization, including yours.

The research supported a model of organizational trust with five key drivers:

- Competence
- Openness and Honesty
- Concern for Employees/Stakeholders
- Reliability
- Identification

Further, our research team learned the five identified drivers were strong and stable predictors of organizational trust across cultures, languages, industries, and types of organizations. The more positive the trust scores for an organization, the more effective the organization was perceived to be and the more satisfied with their jobs employees were. Conversely, lower trust scores predicted lower effectiveness and less job satisfaction. In other words, positive evaluations of each of the five drivers told us (predicted) an organization would receive high trust scores, while negative evaluations of the dimensions resulted in low trust. Importantly, this was true regardless of the background of individuals or the type of organizations they were evaluating. The ability of the five drivers to predict trust scores and the reality that trust scores predict perceived organizational effectiveness and job satisfaction provide a model to address specifically

Figure 2.1 Model of Organizational Trust, Job Satisfaction and Effectiveness*

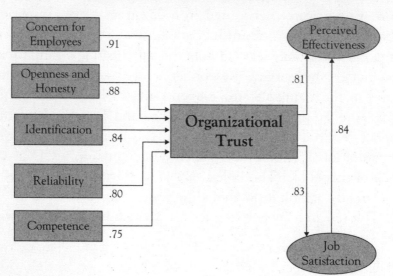

*Numbers indicate statistical significance (p = <.01). Standardized path parameters range from 0 to 1.00. The higher the number, the stronger the dimension is a predictor. Statistical significance at the .01 level means there is only a 1 in 100 chance that the findings were by chance.

trust building. Figure 2.1 shows the exact relationships of the five drivers to trust, job satisfaction, and perceived effectiveness.

The research participants who helped us develop our model, the other research projects we studied, and our own client experiences all point to how complex and variable organizational trust is. One of our study participants summed it up this way:

> "Organizational trust is a lot of things. It is, of course, people, but it is also how we execute, what the competition does, whether we share the values of our leadership, and a lot more. It isn't just my peers and our managers; it is advertising, customer service, quality, and whether we will survive for the future. I frankly don't know where to begin."

It is not surprising that, although most of us can agree that trust is the *main thing*, we have difficulty envisioning a comprehensive approach to trust building. We believe our model meets that challenge and provides the best place to begin. As we now describe each dimension of the trust model, we will provide examples of both trust breaking and trust building.

Dimension One: Competence

"I loved my co-workers. We had the best supervisor ever—but we did not know what we were doing. I left right before the layoffs started."
—*San Francisco, California, survey participant*

The competence dimension is the ability of the organization through its leadership, strategy, decisions, quality, and capabilities to meet the challenges of its environment. Competence relates to the overall efficiency of the organization as well as to the quality of its products or services. Competence comes from the capabilities of employees at all organizational levels. Finally, competence is measured by an organization's ability to achieve its objectives.

Several years ago, one of our long-time clients made the decision to introduce robotics for its assembly line. Employees working the line long had been known for their excellent performance, resulting in high production levels with virtually no quality defects. Programming the robotics technology was a competency none of the current employees possessed. The company debated whether to find other assignments for these high-quality employees or attempt to train them for the pending changes. Leaders highly trusted their employees' abilities in their current assignments. They did not have the same level of confidence that these senior employees could adapt to the new requirements. The employees expressed concern management was trying to get rid of them. They also questioned their own ability to learn a new and challenging technology. By the time the decision was made to offer training, trust levels for both leaders and employees had eroded. Twenty-seven of thirty employees successfully completed the robotics training and the three who were unsuccessful were transferred to other positions. Despite predictions for higher production levels with the new technology, it was three years before the assembly line returned to its prior level of efficiency and quality. We can argue many factors were at play, but lowered trust levels for both leadership and assembly workers surely had a negative impact on the change process. The division manager summed up his experience: "I should have trusted they could learn. The suspicion we brought on by debating what to do cost us dearly. I have learned my lesson that a competent group should be entrusted with new challenges."

Unlike, the airlines we described in Chapter One, Southwest Airlines provides an example of what can happen when management trusts in the competence of its employees. Southwest's operating strategy has always focused on providing low-cost, no-frills service with frequent direct flights. The method for achieving success in using this strategy has been to employ a leadership approach based on trust. While many companies argue that the customer is always right, Southwest executives believe employees come first. As company founder and former CEO Herb Kelleher explains, "Customers are not always right, and I think that is one of the biggest betrayals of your people you can possibly commit. The customer is frequently wrong. We don't carry those sorts of customers. We write them and say, 'Fly somebody else. Don't abuse our people.'"[3]

At Southwest, employees are number-one based on the belief that the way you treat your employees is the way they will treat your customers. This belief in the competence of Southwest employees has produced exceptional levels of customer service. Southwest has consistently been rated by the United States Department of Transportation Consumer Report as having the best on-time performance, best baggage handling, and fewest complaints of all major air carriers. In a highly competitive industry in which all carriers strive to receive top ratings in any of the three reporting categories, Southwest is the only airline to ever be rated best in all three categories—a feat called "the triple crown." Indeed, Southwest once held the triple crown for five consecutive years, an astonishing record considering no other airline has held the triple crown for even one month.[4]

Other key corporate philosophies of Southwest suggest work should be fun (employees are encouraged to take their jobs and the competition seriously—but not themselves) and that employees should do whatever it takes to meet the needs of customers. As Colleen Barrett, the executive vice president for customers, explains, "No employee will ever be punished for using good judgment and good old common sense when trying to accommodate a customer—no matter what our rules are." The results of the Southwest leadership approach have been nothing short of phenomenal. The airline has been rated as one of the nation's ten best companies for which to work. Each year Southwest receives over 200,000 applications for some 4,000 available jobs. The demand for employment at the airline is so great that it is numerically easier to be accepted at Harvard than it is to become a mechanic at Southwest.[5] In an industry plagued by problems associated with excessive costs, frequent labor disputes, and the often-changing whims of travelers, Southwest has been a bastion of profitability. Southwest is the only U.S. airline to have made money every year since 1973.[6]

Competence Dimension: Strategy, decisions, quality, capabilities, leadership, efficiency, effectiveness, achievement of objectives

---

Dimension Two: Openness and Honesty

"I have never felt better about giving it everything
I have. The boss is a straight shooter if I ever saw
one. My previous company kept us in the dark.
This place is entirely different."

—*Sydney, Australia, survey participant*

The openness and honesty dimension is reflected in how organizations communicate about problems, engage in constructive disagreements, and provide input into job-related decisions. Openness and honesty are positively evaluated when managers and supervisors keep confidences and provide information about job performance and evaluation of performance. Employees evaluate an organization as open and honest when they are provided information about how job-related problems are handled and how major organizational decisions will affect them as individuals. Long-term strategic direction available to all employees is a mark of an open and honest organization. Openness and honesty seem straightforward and certainly related to trust. However, over 80 percent of all surveyed organizations report communication problems, with credibility of leadership communication generally rated low. We asked leaders to describe how they communicate to avoid low credibility and build trust.

John Bills, vice president of customer support for the West Zone at Philips Medical Systems told us, "If we can sit with our employees and explain to them what the compelling reasons are for them to perform—how it impacts our business, our customers, and the job—we found as they understood this our employees just took hold of this and began to solve the problem." Reggy P.J. van der Wielen, global R&D programme director, Heart Health, Spreads, and Cooking Products at Unilever, put it another way, "Communicate—communicate—communicate. Be as transparent as possible about intentions and why things are the way they are. Be crystal clear about the intentions. No window dressing! Reward good performance, and do not tolerate poor performance. Stimulate risk taking and accept failure—within reason!"[7]

Mary Jacobus, president and chief operating officer of *The New York Times* Regional Media Group, was responsible for fifteen regional daily newspapers and twenty-four weeklies

diff dynamic in higher ed

mostly located in the southeastern United States.* With fifteen newspaper publishers reporting to her, Mary described her communication and trust-building approach, "My default method for building trust is to be totally honest about what we are facing as a business, how I perceive the performance of others, and being clear about my expectations. I work very hard to eliminate what I would call 'politicism' in the organization so we can work together more effectively. It is a balance. You have to have enough information to communicate to employees so that they have a picture of what is happening in your organization. For example, layoffs. We had round after round of layoffs in our organization, and people want to know, 'Is this the end? Are the layoffs over? Is my job safe?' These are often difficult questions to answer as, at the time you restructure your organization and do layoffs, you are saying this is what we see now and we don't want to eliminate any more positions, but as the economy gets worse we may have to do more. As a result, people are living with a sense of uncertainty that they have never had before.

"So my message has been consistently to say that the people who come out of this with us will have skills that provide true value to the organization, they will have developed their digital skills, and they will skate to where the puck is going to be. Those who will be most successful in the future will be those who can live with uncertainty and who see our changing organizational situation as an opportunity. The people who ask 'Hey, can I have a piece of this action?'

"As a leader I try to anticipate the questions that are on the minds of my employees. It's fairly easy to do that. People want to

---

*Sadly, Mary became ill at work and died just a few weeks after our interview with her. As Janet Robinson, president and CEO of The New York Times, said, "Mary was brilliant, dedicated, focused, and witty. She passionately cared about all those around her and all that she did, personally and professionally. In many ways, she was one of our company's most popular and effective ambassadors for all that we hold dear as an organization."[8]

know: 'Where is this company going; is it true we are going to shut down; are we going to sell this newspaper; what's going to happen with my job; what is happening with our industry; what is our company doing to make itself stronger?' I talk with my publishers every week and try to equip them with as much information as possible because they are the local leaders and they generally provide answers for their employees on a day-to-day-basis."[9]

Openness and Honesty Dimension: Communication about problems, constructive disagreements, job-related decisions, keeping confidences, performance evaluations, job-related problems, decision making, long-term strategic direction

---

Dimension Three: Concern for Employees/ Stakeholders

"They want us to break our backs for them and, if we don't, they think we can be replaced in a heartbeat. Sure the money is good but we are just numbers to management."

—*Denver, Colorado, survey participant*

The concern for employees dimension is squarely about communication and employment practices. For employees to trust the organization has concern for them, they need to believe they are heard. It begins with the immediate supervisor or manager listening to employees and acting on their needs, ideas, or concerns. Trust is related to leaders' attempts to bring information to employees and how leaders talk about any specific employee group to others. The concern dimension is reflected in the perception and reality of top management wanting to communicate regularly with employees and exhibiting a willingness to hear and act on employee concerns. Employees trust the organization when they believe their immediate supervisors or managers are concerned about their personal well-being. Top management is trusted when policies and procedures within the organization reflect concern for the well-being of employees generally. Safety procedures, health plans and benefits, family leave, vacation, performance evaluation, salary scales, promotional practices, and a host of other organization-wide processes determine whether employees trust the organization has concern for their well-being. In Chapter Five, we expand the basics of this dimension to other stakeholders.

The MITRE Corporation, one of the nation's leading non-profit aviation, defense and intelligence, and enterprise modernization research corporations, was rated in 2008 as among the ten best for encouraging balance between the work and personal lives of their employees. For example, employees at The MITRE Corporation are provided with tuition reimbursement up to $20,000 and are given bonuses for earning advanced degrees.[10] Bill Albright, director of quality of work life and benefits for The MITRE Corporation, explains the mutual benefits for the corporation and employees, "We heard from a lot of employees through the years that pursuing education was a goal, but cost and time were obstacles. In response, MITRE developed its Educational Assistance Program, which makes it possible for employees to achieve their professional goals. A great by-product of supporting educational pursuits is that we add to the company's collective knowledge base, so it's truly a win-win situation."[11]

Another organization that has based its leadership approach on concern for employees is Patagonia. When mountaineer Yvon Chouinard founded Patagonia in 1973, he never aspired to be an executive. The business struggled at first, but by the mid-1980s sales began to increase, growing from $20 million to over $100 million by 1990. Today, sales volume at Patagonia is around $250 million per year, and the company makes a wide range of products from outdoor clothing and travel gear to fishing equipment. Despite the growth, Chouinard has held fast to the values of teamwork and camaraderie he enjoyed as a mountaineer. Employees at Patagonia dress as they please (often in t-shirts and shorts, sitting barefoot at their desks); surf when the conditions at nearby beaches are good (the daily surf report is prominently displayed in the lobby of the corporate headquarters, and employees can take advantage of liberal flex-time policies); and enjoy company-sponsored ski and climbing trips, a cafeteria serving high-quality, healthy food (including a wide range of vegetarian options), a subsidized on-site day care center, and the option to take a leave of absence from work for up to two months at a non-profit of their choice while still receiving their full pay from Patagonia. These benefits make the company a highly desirable place of employment—on average some nine hundred people apply for every open position. When Chouinard is at the Patagonia headquarters, he does not have a reserved parking spot (such spots are reserved for those who drive fuel-efficient cars) or special perks or office space; he considers himself no more important than others in the organization.[12] Such treatment would only damage the employee-centric spirit of the company. Chouinard believes: "Finding the right balance between the management problems that come with growth and maintaining our philosophy of hiring independent-minded people and trusting them with responsibility is the key to Patagonia's success."[13]

Concern for Employees/Stakeholders Dimension: Listening to employees, acting on employee ideas, concerns, needs; leadership communication; leadership listening; leadership description of employees, employment policies, and practices

---

Dimension Four: Reliability

"From the president on down, they say the same
thing. You may not always like what they tell you,
but you can count on it. I trust them even when it
isn't good news."

—Rome, Italy, survey participant

The reliability dimension is about keeping commitments and basic follow-through. It is about doing what supervisors and managers say they are going to do. It is about telling all organizational members when something has to change and why. It is consistent behavior from day to day. For top management, reliability is keeping commitments made to the organization and telling the organization the reason if any commitments must change. The reliability dimension of trust should not be confused with sameness or the status quo. Reliability is doing what we say we are going to do and saying why. Often that means communicating about the need for change from the status quo. Reliability also is consistently listening to ideas, issues, and concerns. It is responding to others on a regular basis, whether the response is positive or negative. Reliability is a steadiness in behavior that builds the trust necessary for uncertain times. A reliable organization is a trusted organization because we can count on the organization to do what it says it is going to do.

We always have counseled our clients to be sure that their words and deeds are aligned. Over the years we have observed open-door policies that existed in name only, town hall meetings in which the information presented was not truthful or accurate, and leaders enjoying perks that were not made available to employees. In every case, we have seen the negative impact of these trust-breaking behaviors on overall organizational effectiveness. Similarly, we have observed our clients truly listening to the concerns of employees—whether over seemingly minor issues like lunch breaks or significant matters related to product quality. It was not always possible for the leaders we have worked with to acquiesce to employees, but the leaders who engaged in trust-building behavior listened respectfully, took action when they could, and offered explanations when the desired actions were not possible. Above all, these leaders were consistent in their behavior and applied policies equitably across the board.

Patti Janega, a consultant, trainer, and instructional designer based in Turin, Italy, has worked with a variety of United

Nations (U.N.) agencies for the last sixteen years. She described for us working with a particular U.N. leader who was especially talented at building trust in a complex environment through his consistent and reliable behaviors:

> "I worked with a person at the U.N. who is British; he first brought the idea to the U.N. in the early 1990s, of developing and providing training for the U.N.'s multi-cultural teams working in various countries throughout the world. This man is quiet and initially had to battle for the idea. But because many people trusted him, at a high level all the way to Kofi Annan, he was able to bring his idea to fruition. It took years for him to build a network of support but he did so by being competent and reliable. . . . The reason for our team working so well is that we trusted in the competence and reliability of our leader, and he respected and trusted us. He now has a huge staff, and he started with no staff; he has built trusting relationships with others and the U.N., and its representatives in many countries have benefited from his work."[14]

Our research colleague, Eugen Avram, a psychology faculty member at the University of Bucharest in Romania, conducted interviews in Romania, Bulgaria, Macedonia, France, Spain, Israel, and Nigeria asking about trust and distrust. A Nigerian pharmacist provided an interesting example of the negative consequences of a lack of reliability experienced in a Nigerian pharmaceutical manufacturing company. Although the company's introduction of a new drug was initially successful, product reliability quickly deteriorated, resulting in major customer dissatisfaction. The pharmacist concluded the lack of product reliability was based on market pressures to produce rapidly in response to the initial successful product launch. Further, no reliability standards for the new drug had been set for factory workers and, when asked, factory workers consistently claimed poor and unreliable supervision had contributed to inconsistent manufacturing standards. Not surprisingly, the pharmacist concluded product reliability was fundamental for trust both within and external to the organization.

On a more positive note, a Nigerian research professional responded to questions about reliability by listing her personal parameters for building trust: "(1) Keep your commitments and promises. Do not give your word if you are unsure; (2) Listen. People trust others they believe understand them; (3) Be accessible. Personalized relationships make others feel respected; (4) Cooperate and look for ways to help. It establishes that you will not run from difficulties; (5) Be fair and consistent. People like to work and do business with individuals who are predictable and dependable; and (6) Be accountable."

A quality assurance professional in Israel offered her observations that perceptions of organizational reliability and trust are broken when leaders do not explain major changes in strategy. She specifically described how her employer had set a specific month for salary increases for all employees. A new chief operating officer set a new strategy and delayed all raises to the next fiscal year. No explanation was given for the change. Employee trust was challenged, and employees reported less overall trust in their employer. The merits of the change in strategy are not the issue, but the lack of perceived reliability and lowered trust resulted in increased employee turnover over the next several months.[15]

> **Reliability Dimension:** Commitments, follow-through, steadiness, consistent behaviors, consistent explanations

Dimension Five: Identification

"It is critical for me to share the values of my organization and of the people around me. Work is only a part of my life and I need to feel I am not just earning a living—that's important but not everything."

—*Hong Kong, survey participant*

The identification dimension is the connection between the organization and individual employees most often based on core values. Identification relates to an individual establishing a personal connection with management and peers and, in a more illusive way, with the entire organization. Identification comes when individuals believe their values are reflected in the values the organization exhibits in day-to-day behaviors. It is not surprising that identification or the lack thereof often is directly related to the quality of management-employee relationships. Employees identify with and trust organizations if the organization conducts itself in a way that is closely related to the way employees believe the organization should operate. It is readily apparent that geographically dispersed workers who have little interpersonal contact with management may be challenged to identify with the organization. The importance of identification for trust requires new thinking about trust building in a global environment.

Over the years we have worked in many Hewlett-Packard sites. In our early days working in the company, the HP Way philosophy of company founders Bill Hewlett and Dave Packard was very apparent to us. In those days, HP did not have layoffs (even in times of economic downturn) and the company demonstrated a strong level of commitment and respect for its customers, employees, and the environment. Certainly, market conditions have changed dramatically, but it appears to many observers that the HP of old no longer exists. What led to the demise of many of the tenets of the HP Way? As the company grew, the demands of maintaining the corporate culture were seemingly just too much to bear. As HP progressed from a start-up in a garage in Palo Alto to a global corporation, it became increasingly difficult for leaders to maintain their connection with employees. This unbundling of organizational identification generally occurs gradually and begins with small changes. We recall working with HP groups in the 1990s who told us that the HP Way was starting to fray at the seams under competitive pressure. One small alteration in day-to-day operations exemplified their concerns. For many years HP provided free coffee and donuts for employees every morning. HP staff, including Bill and Dave themselves, would gather each and every morning to share a cup of coffee and a donut and to talk about the latest initiatives at work and family happenings. As the company grew, it was no longer practical to offer this perk to employees, and in the 1990s the coffee and donuts disappeared. This seemingly small change was apocalyptic to many of the long-time HP staffers with whom we talked. To them it signaled the end of an era—the end of the HP Way and the beginning of a transition from a company built on trust and identification with corporate values to a company joining the ranks of so many other less distinctive high-tech companies.

The importance of identification appears much the same across many different cultures. Eugen Avram gathered examples from Romania, Bulgaria, Macedonia, and Spain, all of which demonstrate how trust is based on identifying with the values and goals of the organization, whether for employees or stakeholders. In Romania, an architect, engineer, and IT specialist all agreed supporting and believing in an organization's goals were critical for trust. The architect added an example of distrust. He reported on his work with an organization where the company was extracting raw materials from the natural environment and claiming a quality of ecological rehabilitation employees distrusted. He described how unhappy and distrusting employees became because they doubted the organization's commitment to the region where they valued living for years to come. In Bulgaria, a research professional described her positive trust in her organization because she shared the organization's values for hiring employees with high levels of scientific capabilities. A Macedonian assistant general manager contended that identification contributes to trust building when individual employees and the organization value constant learning, constant improvement, and respect for the competition. A nurse in Spain described how important it was for medical professionals to share a philosophy of quality patient care with medical facility management.[16]

Identification Dimension: Connection to peers, management, the entire organization, values similar to peers, values similar to management

---

Trust and Job Satisfaction and Effectiveness

"We must trust our own thinking. Trust where we're going. And get the job done."

—*Wilma Mankiller, former principal chief of the Cherokee Nation*

In our research, the five dimensions of organizational trust, when working together, were strong predictors of how satisfied people were with their organizations and how effective they saw their organizations. These findings were true whether the organization was large or small, whether it operated in one location or several, and whether it was all in one country or many countries. The findings were true for both profit and non-profit organizations. Of course, we acknowledge we did not have research participants in all parts of the world and in all possible cultures. But the strength of the findings powerfully directed our energies to test the trust model in everyday practice.

We began our quest to better understand the model by returning to the organizations which had participated in our original work. Each organization was provided an individualized report about their specific findings as contrasted to all organizations in the study. We talked with leadership and study participants to ask whether we were making sense from their perspectives. (We knew we were making research sense, but we wanted to see whether managers and workers could relate to our findings.) The response was overwhelming. One CEO said it best: "I can name it now—I have known for years trust is the basic of our success. I could not put my finger on it. Our identification scores were off the charts positive compared to others. I have worked on this for over twenty-five years. I have talked about values at every opportunity. We talk about values when we hire people, when we work with our customers, and when we experience problems. I also think these values guide the way in which we treat all the people who work here. I am convinced this model makes a contribution to all who want to think more comprehensively about improving their effectiveness."

Line workers told us they could now understand why they were happy or unhappy with their current work situations. Equally important, one human resources vice president said, "I can do something with this. It not only makes sense, but it can influence my practice."

Next, we began to use the model with many of our clients. The results are why we are writing this book. The model provides practical direction with measurable results. What we learned and what our clients learned are the subjects of the next five chapters. For each of our five dimensions, we describe both high-trust and low-trust examples in real organizations. We begin the practical process of building trust in each of the dimensions: *competence, openness and honesty, concern for employees, reliability, and identification.*

Chapter Lessons in Trust

1. Trust is the main thing.

2. Organizational trust has five dimensions: competence, openness and honesty, concern for employees/stakeholders, reliability, and identification.

3. Organizational competence is the ability to meet environmental challenges and objectives.

4. Organizational openness and honesty is the communication ability of the organization to provide needed information and engage in constructive exchanges at all levels.

5. Organizational concern for employees/stakeholders is squarely about communication and employment practices.

6. Organizational reliability is keeping commitments and explaining the "why" of change, not just supporting the status quo.

7. Organizational identification occurs when individual and organizational values are similar and connect individuals and organizations.

8. Organizational trust predicts job satisfaction and perceived organizational effectiveness.

9. Competence, openness and honesty, concern for employees, reliability, and identification predict trust across cultures, organizational types and sizes, languages, and worker locations.

10. The research-based trust model is practical and produces results.

Part Two

UNDERSTANDING THE FIVE DIMENSIONS OF TRUST

"The mission is run on trust . . . and when everything
went wrong for Apollo 13 that trust paid off."
—*Gene Kranz, retired NASA mission
director who, during the Apollo 13 explosion
crisis in 1970, was instrumental in making the
decision to slingshot the craft around the moon,
resulting in a successful return to earth.*

In Part Two, we devote a chapter to each of the five dimensions of our organizational trust model: competence, openness, concern, reliability, and identification. For each of the dimensions, we describe what happens when trust is high and when distrust is present in any organization. We address how to approach building trust for each dimension. Importantly, we share what we have learned from personal interviews with leaders who address each of the five trust dimensions. Part Two is designed to assist organizations in applying the trust model by learning from both the good and bad experiences of others.

3

TRUST AND ORGANIZATIONAL COMPETENCY

"A competent leader can get efficient service from
poor troops while, on the contrary, an incapable
leader can demoralize the best of troops."
—John J. Pershing, *general of the Armies of the*
United States of America, 1860–1948

There is an almost endless range of possibilities for what can be used to describe competent organizations. Popular descriptors include terms such as best place to work, industry leader, most profitable, most efficient, fast-growing, leading innovator, family-friendly, respected leadership, high-quality products, service excellence, or visionary. While the terms make for good media coverage, most would agree the enduring nature of the competent organization is complex and varied.

The Competent Organization

One of our clients recently told us a story that effectively illustrates organizational competency. "Just surviving as we shifted to manufacturing in Malaysia illustrated our core excellence. We had run high-quality manufacturing plants in the U.S. for over fifty years. Our labor costs were way too high for our global markets. We either had to change or die. I mean that. None of us wanted the change. We had to figure out what to do with our current employees and yet move quickly. We did not want layoffs, and we were able to create good early retirement incentives. But it was hard. Our employees trusted us throughout the process because we told an unpleasant truth. We made the case

47

for change and we made change. We had a rough year or two, but we have come out on the other side with increased market share and are profitable again. Being competent does not mean it isn't hard. It does mean you take needed action." Our client's example illustrates the difficulty with describing all of the possible ways to understand competence. It also focuses our thinking on the key characteristics for becoming and staying competent.

We believe *purpose* and *vision* are the basis for competence. Purpose and vision are the *"what"* justifying organizational existence, the foundation for aspirations, structure, strategy, goals, and leadership. Purpose and vision reflect values and beliefs about what is important and what should become the bedrock of organizational culture. Any discussion of organizational competence is incomplete without understanding how purpose and vision are developed and implemented.

Harvard University professor John Kotter defines vision as a concise statement of the direction in which a group or organization and its people are headed. To be compelling, a vision must be *desirable* and *attainable*—meaning the vision must both motivate and inspire followers and be achievable to those in the organization. He goes on to explain an effective vision is specific enough to provide real guidance to people, yet vague enough to encourage initiative and remain relevant under a variety of conditions. Visions that are too specific can serve to demotivate once results are achieved. A well-conceived vision provides an over-arching philosophy or value orientation for the group or organization.[1]

We believe vision serves four core purposes. First, *vision motivates and inspires*. Vision statements set the bar for organizational performance by providing lofty goals that encourage extraordinary performance. Vision statements like those at the Girl Scouts of the USA ("Girl Scouting builds girls of courage, confidence, and character, who make the world a better place") or Unilever ("To add vitality to life. We meet the everyday needs for nutrition, hygiene, and personal care with brands that help people feel good, look good, and get more out of life") encourage employees to get excited about the purpose of the organization where they are working—building a more unified commitment to the overall company vision.

Second, *vision guides action*. Vision informs members of the organization how they are expected to behave. At Amazon.com employees are encouraged to follow the vision to be "Earth's most customer-centered company." At Southwest Airlines the vision is "to provide the highest quality of Customer Service delivered with a sense of warmth, friendliness, individual pride, and company Spirit" (with the irregular capitalization emphasizing the most important dimensions). These vision statements inform employees what is expected and encourage creativity in meeting customer needs. Given the direction strong vision statements provide, it is no surprise that both Amazon.com and Southwest Airlines have consistently been rated by *BusinessWeek* as among its customer service champions, with Amazon.com earning the top spot in 2009.[2]

Third, *vision statements should be simple and to the point*. An effective vision should be short enough for members of the organization to remember. We believe if organizational members cannot recall and recite the vision, then, in practice, it does not exist. We have observed many organizations with lengthy vision statements posted on the corporate office walls. When we ask employees what their organization's vision is, they usually can only remember one or two phrases at best. Lengthy visions do not motivate or inspire because they are too complicated to guide action. Motivating visions are simple and to the point. Compare the Disney vision ("We create happiness)" to the vision of the now failed Kemper Insurance company ("To gather, manage, and protect the assets of individual, corporate, and institutional clients—generating attractive returns and long-term appreciation for our clients and stockholders by developing and distributing high-quality products and services and operating in a professional and ethical manner"). It is not surprising Disney employees have a clear sense of commitment and purpose, while those at Kemper reportedly struggled to identify with their vision.

Finally, *vision should operate on multiple levels*. In large organizations, one singular vision often is not relevant to employees at all levels within the company. Our work at Bristol-Myers Squibb provides a good example. While the corporate vision ("To extend and enhance human life by providing the highest quality health and personal care products") is effective because it motivates and inspires, guides action, and is short enough to remember, it does not touch every job function in the organization. We worked with customer service representatives who were responsible for taking orders for Bristol-Myers Squibb products. These employees were guided by their own vision ("To be perceived by all of our customers as the preeminent provider of outstanding, quality service"). Further, employees in this department worked in teams, each with its own vision (For example: "To maintain a partnership committed to providing superior customer service— fulfilling all expectations with professionalism and respect"). Each of these visions aligned to the core purpose of the larger organization but also seemed to fulfill the more level-specific needs of various employees in the organization.[3]

A distinctive vision is important for building organizational trust. As Angelique Rewers, president and owner of Bon Mot Communications, explains, "An organization that wants to establish trust with its employees, investors, and customers must start with a sure sense of what defines it. It must know why it exists to begin with and what makes it uniquely different from every other organization in the marketplace. Take, for example, Ethos Water, which identifies itself as a brand with a social mission, to help children around the world get clean water and raise awareness of the world water crisis. The company's vision is printed on every bottle of water it sells, thereby reminding consumers that a portion of the purchase price goes toward its goal of donating $10 million to clean water programs by 2010. Ethos Water's vision not only gives consumers a feeling of doing good, but it also gives every employee motivation for delivering added value to the organization."[4]

Leadership, of course, is closely related to purpose and vision. Leaders help to establish direction, inherit the direction of predecessors, and continually assess purpose and vision in relationship to an ever-changing environment. Often leaders are evaluated more for the direction they set than for their personal characteristics. Our research, along with the work of many others, supports the fact that leadership is described along a competence to incompetence continuum both within the organization and by external stakeholders. Interestingly enough, only close associates evaluate leaders for their individual competence. The competence of organizational leadership is much more often determined in response to achievement of organizational goals and the ability to adapt to prepare for the future.

We had an opportunity to meet Frances Hesselbein when she was honored by the International Leadership Association in November 2008. Once a volunteer Girls Scout troop leader and later the USA CEO of the Girl Scouts and a U.S. Presidential Medal of Freedom recipient, Hesselbein epitomizes what we have been saying about vision and leadership. Hesselbein told us directly that leadership is a matter of "how to be, not how to do."[5] Hesselbein spoke about being mission-focused, values-based, and demographics-driven. She helped us understand the competent leader helps to move people forward, not contain them. People follow when they trust.

Goals, strategy, structure, and *execution* also contribute to the competence profile of any organization. Is it clear how purpose and vision translate into goals? Does strategy support ambitious goals? Does the structure of the organization support or retard performance? Is structure historic or performance-driven? What about execution? What does the record of achievement look like? Some organizations with strong past records of achievement are viewed as marginally competent because they are slow to adapt to changing circumstances. Others with limited past results are evaluated as competent based on assessments of future potential. Comparisons among organizations with similar purposes and objectives are inevitable from stockholders, the investment community, customers, donors, regulators, and employees. Competence is both an individual organizational assessment and an assessment made among peer organizations.

The competence evaluation for structure and execution deserves a special explanation. Achievement of goals and evaluation of strategy are subject to both internal and external stakeholder scrutiny. However, structure and execution are more likely to be of concern to internal constituents or those connected directly to the structure and execution of the organization such as vendors. External stakeholders (customers, investors, donors, and others) more often view structure and execution from the perspective of whether their needs are met and goals are achieved. There is less concern for the *how* and more emphasis on results. Internally, structure and execution are evaluated for whether goals make sense and whether ambitious performance expectations are supported and realistic. Structure is related to organizational control systems that facilitate or retard effectiveness. A hierarchical chain of command, team-based networks, or matrix designs all represent structure decisions about who decides and who will make the final decisions. Execution is the day-to-day operation within a given structure in support of goals and strategy. Visible success or failure outcomes result from the execution competence of the organization.

We return again to Philips Medical Systems for an example of successful integration of goals and strategy with solid execution. John Bills, vice president of customer support for the West Zone at Philips Medical Systems, described for us the need to establish new goals, strategy, and plans for execution in order to solve a major problem with field change orders (FCOs) on Philips Imaging Systems found in hospitals and clinics around the world. Field change orders are factory modifications and updates to repair software glitches or problematic parts on

Philips Imaging Systems such as CT scanners, MRI machines, and Cardiac Catheterization Laboratory equipment. The factory sends out change orders and gives customer support personnel a prescribed amount of time to complete the FCOs. Bills knew the FCOs were not a priority for customer support personnel, who were more focused on fixing broken equipment than on performing routine maintenance and upgrades. Bills established a goal to transition customer service from a "break-fix" mentality to a customer-focused approach. Bills identified a straightforward strategy without adding additional rules or management oversight. He simply explained the core need to complete FCOs in a timely manner. He organized his field service engineers into Customer Care Teams (CCTs) and assigned a "champion" within each team. The champion had ownership for ensuring all FCOs were completed as scheduled by the factory. Execution was in the hands of nineteen teams and their champions. The nineteen CCTs were soon sharing best practices and competing to get all of the FCOs done. The results demonstrate the point. Prior to establishing the new goals and strategy, as many as five hundred or six hundred FCOs were regularly coming due or were past due. For over three years following implementation of the new approach to goals, strategy, and execution, not a single FCO has been past due in the West Zone. Based on the FCO success, Bills extended this approach to planned maintenance (PM) scheduling. Historically about 60 percent of the PMs in Bills' West Zone had been completed on time. Each Customer Care Team (CCT) now has a PM "champion" who is trusted to manage this work. Execution again was designed to support the changed goals and strategy. Today, in Bills' West Zone, 98 percent of the planned maintenance is completed on time, a 38 percent improvement. Bills values this progress because, as a forty-one-year veteran in the medical systems business, he knows factory change orders and planned maintenance, when completed on time, directly contribute to fewer emergency breakdowns and to both customer and employee satisfaction.[6]

Core capabilities represent another contributor to the competence equation. What are organizational strengths? How are they represented? Importantly, how are core capabilities maintained and strengthened? Hiring, evaluation, promotional processes, training, education, and organizational learning are designed to develop core capabilities. Continuous improvement processes—both human and technological—enhance strengths. The flip side of strengths and core capabilities is, of course, weakness, vulnerability, and challenge. The competent organization understands both and develops strategies to preserve the best while addressing or minimizing the negative.

Unilever Director Reggy P.J. van der Wielen provides a personal example of core capability development, "In the second half of 2002, after having worked as an R&D project leader at the Unilever Health Institute for about three years, I indicated to my boss that I felt ready for a new challenge. He had the same opinion and, as it turned out, I was the preferred candidate to take on a department director role at the Institute. There were about sixty people in the group I would be responsible for leading, and there was more growth in headcount predicted. Although my experience in resource leadership was limited, I was selected for this role on the basis of my technical competency. My superiors in the organization exhibited confidence in my ability to develop into a resource leader. My boss and I both acknowledged that this new position would require a steep learning curve. As a result, I was offered the help of an independent external leadership coach. This supported me by providing a sounding board to help me in defining approaches for managing and developing my direct reports, many of whom were peers before my promotion. At the same time, having an external leadership coach offered me the opportunity to interact with an independent professional from outside the company whom I could safely communicate with about any uncertainties in my new role. The outcome was an acceleration of my personal development as a resource leader, which undoubtedly was also to the benefit of the organization."[7] We have seen the other side of van der Wielen's story in countless organizations in which we have worked as consultants. Too often technically competent individuals are promoted into leadership roles without adequate training or support. These new leaders often fail to enlist support and to build trust within their teams and departments. This is not because they are not capable and motivated, but rather because they have not been provided with the tools necessary to develop their core capabilities as trusted leaders.

Change is the final component of competency we will discuss. We know, as Thomas Friedman has so aptly described, "the world is flat" with our playing fields local, global, networked, and interdependent.[8] Past organizational wisdom is subject to revision with few proven strategies for navigating unprecedented turbulence. It is not whether organizations are going to change, it is how, when, and with what result. In the not-so-distant past, the avoidance of crisis was a mark of organizational competence. Today, leadership during crisis is the new standard for competence. It is change management, risk and crisis response, and an ever-increasing understanding of complex environments. It is the generation of a trusted steadiness during turbulence that has become the new mark for effective organizations.

Many are surprised to learn that an engineer at Kodak, Steven Sasson, developed the prototype for the digital camera in 1975. At the time Kodak was the world leader in celluloid film sales and company executives were reluctant to cut into market share of its many successful products such as film stock and processing, Kodachrome color slides, and Instamatic cameras. After Sasson's pioneering efforts, Kodak engineers continued to explore digital imaging, amassing over one thousand patents. By the early 1990s, as many other companies were on the verge of developing digital cameras, executives at Kodak were unceasing in their focus on film, a market which the company had dominated for so long. Despite the fact that almost all digital photography relies on inventions patented by Kodak engineers, Kodak's 2007 market share for digital cameras was just 8.8 percent—well behind Canon and Sony. As a result, Kodak has been forced to shed more than two-thirds of its workforce as the sales of film have plummeted. Kodak was a company populated with brilliant engineers who exhibited tremendous technical savvy, yet those at the top demonstrated a lack of competence in analyzing changing consumer preferences. The result is a once-powerful icon now struggles to hold share in the crowded photographic marketplace.[9]

Peter Stark, managing principal of Chaos Navigation and a faculty member in the Augsburg Helsinki School of Management and at the Institute of Management in Berlin, summed up for us the present change imperative, "Today's business environment is characterized by waves of change and chaos. A need exists for change competence that is related to trust. The only source of competitive advantage for global organizations is the ability of an organization's collective human assets to outthink, out-learn, and out-create other organizations. Trust in the organization is necessary to accomplish any of these activities."[10]

We don't claim the competence factors we describe are the only ways competence can be understood. We do believe, however, that purpose and vision, leadership, goals, strategy, structure, execution, core capabilities, and change are central to the evaluations made about whether to trust or distrust organizational competence. In support of our perspective, we now describe what happens when there is trust or distrust in competence.

Trust in Competence

"Obscurity and competence—that is the life that is best worth living."

—*Mark Twain, American author and satirist, 1835–1910*

Many engage in the pitfall of assuming because they personally believe in the competence of their organizations that others share their trust. However, *being competent and having others trust in competence is not the same thing. Being competent is fundamental; having others trust in competence is equally important.* One of our clients provided us a wonderful example. Our client was a medical products software developer. Products primarily were sold to large hospital systems needing both standardized and customized software applications. Our client's reputation rested on the success of customized products. Their standardized programs were viewed as acceptable but not exceptional. Based on profit margins, our client determined he must increase sales in standardized applications.

First, our client increased expenditures in research and development to improve the standardized programs. Next, the organization set ambitious goals for sales increases and expanded the sales force to help meet the new targets. After a year, leaders were dismayed to realize that, while sales had increased to the dollar amount targeted, the volume was mainly attributed to customized applications. Profit goals were not achieved. We were asked to interview both sales force members and selected customers. What we discovered was not surprising. Objectively, the quality of the new standardized applications had improved significantly. The sales force was well trained and the new marketing materials were both accurate and attractive. However, the approach did not take into account long-term customer perceptions of where the organization's true capabilities were. Too little emphasis was placed on acquainting customers with how robust the new standardized applications were as contrasted to past products and how the range of applications available could rival what had previously been available only in customized products. Our client had not thoughtfully understood the competence perception of their customer base. Customers held in high regard, (that is, trusted) the customized products but did not have the type of information they needed to extend that trust to the new standardized product line.

New marketing materials and a revised sales approach increased sales over the following year. The products were the same, but our client came to understand how complex and important it was to address squarely perceptions of competence leading to the trust necessary to make the purchase decision. One sales force member summed it up, "I could not have imagined saying to a customer that we were not very good at standardized applications and now we were. I learned I needed to explain why we had become so good at something we had not done well in the past. It worked, but it was not what I would normally have done."

It is relatively easy to believe trust in the competence of an organization contributes importantly to the success of sales and marketing. Customer loyalty is a critical ingredient to long-term positive results. What is not as readily understood is that trust in the competence of an organization actually contributes to the competence of the organization. High-quality potential employees are attracted to organizations they believe are on the leading edge, get results, are innovative, and have bright futures. High-quality potential employees have choices. They choose organizations in which they trust the competence of leadership in the ability to vision and set goals and strategy in pursuit of vision. Additionally, current employees are more innovative when they believe their ideas will meet with a fair and competent evaluation. Both employees and customers exhibit more loyalty to organizations with competent track records. In fact, a reputation for competence is crucial to dealing with the inevitable challenges of organizational life.

Distrust in Competence

"When you have a low level of trust you pay attention to all of the details."

—*Anonymous bank employee*

Bad things happen when distrust in competence is present. Practical experience and research both support the damage done when key stakeholders distrust the competence of an organization.[11] We have known for many years that customer brand loyalty is reduced when product quality is perceived to be low. In highly competitive technology markets, repeat customer business is linked to the perceived competence of service support. Non-profit organizations lose donor support when basic capabilities are in question. What has been more recently discovered is that employee commitment to an organization is directly related to perceptions of organizational competence. Employees' belief in the competence of their organization is a prerequisite to employee commitment necessary for long-term success. For example, employees who do not believe their organization is competent are more likely to withhold important information from others in the organization. In other words, *distrust in competence compromises the ability of an organization to collaborate whether in face-to-face interaction or in virtual environments.*

An example occurred in late 2006 when the new Airbus A380, the world's largest passenger jet, took to the sky for the first time with a full load of passengers. The seven-hour test flight of the 308-ton super jumbo that can carry up to 555 passengers was an aeronautical triumph. But when the plane (larger than a Boeing 747) touched down near the Airbus factory in southern France, questions began to surface about the viability of the aircraft in the wake of massive delivery delays to customers around the world. What had originally been announced as a six-month delay in the manufacture of the aircraft ultimately pushed back delivery dates two full years, leading major customers such as Arab Emirates and FedEx to cancel orders—resulting in the potential loss of billions of dollars in revenue for Airbus.[12] The reasons for the delay were complex—the result of the intricacies of leading a multi-national operation with manufacturing sites across Europe with French, German, British, and Spanish stakeholders. Yet, when the problems with the A380 were investigated, Airbus executives acknowledged the primary reason for the delay was that the design software used in factories in Germany and France was not compatible. As inconceivable as it sounds, engineers in Germany and France were using different versions of the CAD-CAM software critical to allowing design specs to be transferred easily back and forth between the two locations. When the bundles of cabin wire arrived in France, workers had difficulty fitting the wires into the airplane fuselage. They tried to pull the wires apart and rethread them through the aircraft, but that proved to be impractical. Ultimately, Airbus was forced to invest in new software to correct the wiring design.[13] Why hadn't the engineers in Germany and France confirmed that the more than three hundred miles of internal electrical wiring built in Hamburg, Germany, would fit properly into the plane on the assembly line in Toulouse, France? Because the teams in both locations insisted on working independently, distrusting the contributions of their counterparts.

Another example reflecting the serious consequences of distrust comes from one of our clients. Our client was experiencing rising product defects in a manufacturing plant long known for a tradition of excellence. Management of the plant had recently changed, but the line workforce had been relatively stable. We were asked to interview both management and workers to determine what was contributing to the quality problem. We discovered an issue of distrust not characteristic of the culture of our client. Line workers had informed management of defects in some of the parts shipped from a vendor new to our client. The new plant manager challenged workers about the accuracy of their information and informed them he would personally investigate. Somewhat accidentally, the night shift line supervisor discovered the son-in-law of the plant manager was the sales manager for the vendor. In fact, the plant manager had ordered a change to this vendor shortly after arriving at his new job. The shift supervisors no longer believed they could work with the plant manager to resolve the defects problem. When we discussed the issue with the plant manager, he assured us he was working with the new vendor to correct the problem and had chosen them for their pricing advantage. Over a six-month period following the initial defects problems, the night shift supervisor and two of his best employees requested transfers to other divisions. They were not specific about their reasons for wanting to transfer, but we believe distrust in the competence and integrity of the plant manager was a major factor. Although the defects problem was corrected, overall plant productivity declined over the next eighteen months. Here are a few more ways that distrust may affect perceptions of organizational competence.

Fairness is equated with organizational competence. Employees who believe they are fairly treated by personnel policies and practices are more likely to highly evaluate the competence of their organization than are those who question the basic justice of processes that directly affect them, such as performance review. Additionally, employees who distrust the competence of their organization are more likely to seek employment elsewhere. High turnover rates are often linked to distrust in competence.

Fear of change is increased when competence is questioned. Both internal and external stakeholders may know that change is inevitable, but they are more likely to resist a particular plan, idea, or course of action if they question the competence of those setting direction. In the worst case, fear of change coupled with low trust contributes to an "us versus them" mentality, making productive change difficult if not impossible. Low trust or outright distrust contributes to problem avoidance, emotional resistance, sabotage, and a host of other dysfunctional outcomes.

We have encountered many situations in organizations in which distrust in the competence of a leader has had adverse consequences, not only for the leader in question, but for the entire team or organization. We observed one situation deteriorate to the point at which two managers, each questioning the competence of the other, would barely speak to one another. This created tension among their direct reports and made it almost impossible for the organization to coordinate even the most mundane day-to-day tasks. The situation reached a critical point as the organization prepared to launch a major change initiative. Our assessment was that, unless the relationship between the two managers could be improved, the changes could not be implemented. Indeed, it was only after one of the managers left the organization that the project began to gain traction.

Few set out to generate distrust in competence, yet distrust is more common than most would like to admit. So what can be done? Next we focus on how to begin trust building important for the competence dimension of our model.

Building Trust in Competence

"If a leader demonstrates competency, genuine
concern for others, and admirable character, people
will follow."
—*T. Richard Chase, folktale author, 1904–1988*

We hope we have convinced you by now that trust is the *main thing* for all types of organizational effectiveness and that understanding how competence is perceived is key to any organization's trust profile. The question then is, "*Why do so many high-integrity, trustworthy leaders fail to build trust in the competence of their organizations?*" We put that question to several senior leaders representing differing types of organizations. Here is what they had to say[14]:

"Most leaders view trust as a competency of the individual versus a capability of the organization. I don't think they view it as an organizational level phenomenon, which then stops them from paying attention to organizational practices/beliefs that support or hinder trust. Also, trust falls into the 'soft' side of leadership, which doesn't always get valued or attention." *Laura Quinn, Ph.D., portfolio manager, Center for Creative Leadership*

"In my opinion, it is not merely the top leaders themselves who matter but the entire layer of top management. The very best of leaders fail in execution when they are shielded from current realities both within the organization and outside the organization.

Maybe it is short-term priorities or maybe the group surrounding the top leader is not sincere in conveying truthful information to the top leadership. Another aspect that contributes to failure in building trust is that, while top leaders may be of high integrity, the executives who surround this power center get tempted to exploit their positions of power. If a top leader cannot keep a check on those closest to him or her, it can be perceived by the organization as tacit acceptance of the deviations by the top leaders. This is an ingredient of failure in building trust." *Former head of an automotive plant in India*

"Leaders fail because they are surrounded by sycophancy and incompetence. When leaders do not exercise fair judgment in choosing subordinates, they pay the cost of being partial and biased. When they become leaders, they look upon positioning those whom they have known in comfortable organizational slots so that their own authority remains unquestioned. An ethically wrong system feeds on itself until there is nothing left to feed on and then it collapses." *Rajeev Kumar, Ph.D., senior practice consultant, Tata Management Training Centre, India*

"They don't see trust as a priority. They have other priorities—like obtaining profit without caring too much about their employees." *Romanian engineer*

"Because they forget to be team leaders, they play on an individual level and lose the big picture." *Macedonian assistant manager*

"Perhaps because they depend too much on their own personal trustworthiness and do not realize they need to delegate and create structures that transmit such trustworthiness to the entire organization." *Spanish translator*

"Too many business and government leaders suffer from delusions of grandeur—an arrogance that leads them to make decisions or behave in such a way that ultimately destroys all trust in their organizations." *Angelique Rewers, president, Bon Mot Communications*

"I think it is because some people are just not meant to be leaders." *Israeli craftsperson*

We were intrigued but not surprised by these answers to our question. The perspectives of the leaders we interviewed for this book, our past research and work with our own clients, and the research of others have helped us frame the strategies we now present for building trust in competence. These are not the only strategies an organization can or should employ, but the strategies we present are tested for their ability to improve perceptions of organizational competence. From this point forward, we will be describing how action, behavior, and communication are interrelated processes necessary for trust building. Being competent is insufficient to be perceived as competent. Being perceived as competent is insufficient to be competent. These are not plays on words. Action, behavior, and communication together build trust in competence.

Strategies for Building Trust in Competence

Before we move to specific strategies, it is important to restate the obvious. We are not suggesting any organization attempt to present itself as competent if it is not. *Core competence is fundamental and is the most important strategy on which to build trust in competence.*

Strategy One: Assess Competence and Trust in Competence

Conduct a complete and thoughtful assessment of the current state of the competence of the organization and the trust evaluation of stakeholders in that competence.

The assessment requires asking key questions and committing to listen and act on the answers. Key questions include:

1. Is our purpose and vision clear and relevant to our current environment?

2. Are our leaders capable of supporting our vision? Do key stakeholders trust in leadership competence?

3. Do we set realistic, yet ambitious goals? Do key stakeholders trust in our goals?

4. Does our strategy support our goals? Do key stakeholders trust in our strategy?

5. Is our structure supporting our goals? Do key stakeholders trust we have a supportive structure?

6. Do we execute effectively and efficiently? Do key stakeholders trust we are effective and efficient?

7. Do we know our strengths and weaknesses? Do key stakeholders trust in our strengths and trust we can improve our weaknesses?

8. Do we respond effectively to change, crisis, and challenge? Do key stakeholders trust in our ability to change and to meet crises and challenges effectively?

9. Where are we strong?

10. What needs to change?

Strategy Two: Assess Purpose and Vision

Pay attention to purpose and vision.

Examine the current purpose and vision of the organization. Evaluate the stated and implied purpose of the organization for its ability to generate a clear and compelling reason for the organization's existence. Evaluate the stated and implied vision for its ability to support the purpose by linking it to the present and future. Ask the following questions:

1. Is the purpose compelling and elevating?

2. Is the purpose relevant?

3. Is the vision clear? Is the vision compelling and elevating? Is the vision supportive of purpose? Is the vision future-oriented?

4. Do key stakeholders understand the relationship of purpose and vision to the daily activities and results of the organization?

Paying attention to purpose and vision is more than generating vision statements and brand promises. It is the continuous examination of how purpose and vision are supported by core values, leadership, goals, strategy, structure, execution, core capabilities, change, and results. As we mentioned earlier in this chapter, it is critical that groups and organizations live the vision by making the vision "real" for everyone. We have helped many organizations develop strategies for doing this by facilitating discussions regarding the behavioral expectations, or norms, which will be used to make the vision real for members of the organization. For example, when organizations have visions emphasizing customer satisfaction, employees must be empowered to meet customer's needs without fear they will later be questioned for their actions. The behavioral expectations at Disney provide a useful illustration. Disney empowers all employees (known as cast members) to provide immediate customer service support to all customers (known as guests). This support, known as "guest recovery," empowers cast members to offer whatever incentives are necessary to uphold the Disney vision of creating happiness. To provide such service, employees must be empowered to make decisions without management approval. An astonishing indication of the depth of employee empowerment at Disney is the fact that customer service representatives, the people who take the tickets at the theme park entrances, have $500,000 in tickets and cash at their disposal to give out to guests who lose or forget their tickets, run out of money, or encounter any other problem.[15]

Strategy Three: Assess Leadership

Excel at leading.

Building trust in competence requires a sometimes harsh assessment of the quality of organizational leaders. Jim Collins, in his famous best-seller, *Good to Great,* has described this assessment as getting the right people on the bus and the wrong people off.[16] He goes so far as to claim you can't really develop excellent purpose and vision until the core competence of leadership is in place. We agree. Although Collins does not specifically refer to trust, our research (and the work of others) links trust in top leaders with the achievement of purpose and vision and bottom-line results. Few would question that it is the responsibility of leaders to form the most effective team possible. So what goes wrong? Several possibilities are worthy of consideration. Many organizations promote leaders based on seniority without thoughtful consideration for individual competency or development. Others never promote from within and look for top industry names who may or may not be a fit with the purpose, vision, and culture of a particular organization. Still others fail to make changes when results clearly lag behind expectations. Of significant importance is the balance of competencies within leadership teams. Is the circle of advisors trusted to challenge, support, change, and bring differing perspectives to key decisions? Finally, excelling at leadership requires leaders to publicly take responsibility and exhibit accountability.

Eaton's of Canada, the once-proud icon of Canadian retail, founded by Timothy Eaton in 1869, is an example of the important role of leadership competence. Timothy Eaton won over Canadians by promoting unparalleled variety in product selection, providing a high level of service, and instituting a money-back guarantee on all purchases. He rewarded employees for their contributions through shares in the company and other benefits not typical of the times, including a reduction in the standard work week. The Eaton's chain grew and flourished for several decades beyond its founder's death in 1910. By the 1930s, Eaton's accounted for an astounding 58 percent of all Canadian retail sales. Through a series of leadership succession decisions beginning in the late 1960s, excellence was eroded, with both employees and customers losing trust in the organization. In 1994 Wal-Mart arrived in Canada, and by 1996 Eaton's had fallen to fifth in market share in Canadian retail behind Wal-Mart, Zeller's, Sears, and The Bay. By 2000 Eaton's ceased to operate as an independent company and was bought out by Sears for $60 million. What led to such a precipitous decline? As Peter Sharpe, executive vice president of Cadillac Fairview Corp., Eaton's largest landlord before its demise, suggests, "It [Eaton's] had been run for a long time by people who don't know anything about merchandising." Former TD banker Robin Korthals adds, "Eaton's had weak management for forty years. If you stacked up the Eaton boys [the decedents of founder Timothy Eaton] against U.S. retail CEOs, it was no contest.[17]

Strategy Four: Design Organizational Architecture for Results

Produce superior results. Design an organizational architecture to facilitate achievement of ambitious goals, focused strategy, appropriate structure, and excellent execution.

Leaders and management design the processes that produce the results of the organization—whether the results are good or bad. We call this the architecture of results. Stakeholders trust organizations that produce high-quality results. Whether results are profit, high-quality service, innovation, quality of products, contribution to broad social issues, or a host of other measures, organizations producing results enjoy trust and confidence. Trust and confidence, in turn, contribute to better long-term performance. Leaders are squarely responsible for this dimension of competence trust building and should ask these questions:

1. Do our goals make sense to support our purpose and vision?
2. Are those goals ambitious and achievable?
3. Are those responsible for goal execution appropriately involved in goal development and implementation?
4. How is strategy developed?
5. Who is involved?

Many organizations with strong purpose and vision fail to regularly examine whether control structures continue to make sense. Technology has changed the way we do everything. Even with massive investments in technology, many organizations have failed to examine how controls and changes in structure should respond to expanding virtual capabilities. Changing work designs—and even location of work—have become subjects for competence evaluation and competitive strategy.

Execution is the final component of the architecture of results. Producing excellent results requires regular examination and updating of policies and procedures, ranging from hiring, performance review, and compensation to internal and external communication planning. Johnsonville Foods is one of the best examples we know of designing an architecture for results. Ralph Stayer joined his family's sausage-making business in Sheboygan, Wisconsin, after graduating from the University of Notre Dame in 1965. In 1978, he replaced his father as president of Johnsonville Foods. Stayer inherited a stable company with annual growth averaging around 20 percent. Johnsonville was a successful company by all accounts, yet Stayer sensed problems. He noticed that workers were operating far below their potential and that many employees appeared disinterested in the company. Most who worked at Johnsonville Foods appeared to be doing no more than meeting minimum performance expectations. Few seemed concerned with excelling in their work. Stayer felt there had to "be a better way" and he became inspired to revolutionize the organizational architecture at Johnsonville Foods. In 1982, Stayer wrote a six-page letter to his employees. The structure at Johnsonville Foods was going to change. Employees would be asked to take far more responsibility for the work they performed. Further, the compensation system would be overhauled. Instead of across-the-board annual raises, employees would be paid for performance. Those who learned new skills and developed their talents would receive the largest salary increases and profit-sharing bonuses.

The traditional organizational structure was dismantled. First-line employees were organized into self-directed work teams. These employees, known as "members," were given a wide array of responsibilities, ranging from budgeting, scheduling, quality control, and marketing to strategic planning and personnel, including the hiring *and* firing of their fellow team members. Middle managers, formerly responsible for the tasks turned over to the first-line workers, now focused their efforts on teaching and on coaching members to lead themselves. Meanwhile, Ralph Stayer turned his attention away from the day-to-day operation of Johnsonville Foods and began to focus more energy on maintaining his leadership philosophy based on trust. Slowly, members working on the production line began to take over more of the responsibility for operating Johnsonville Foods.

The watershed moment came in 1985 when Johnsonville was asked to produce a new line of meats for another manufacturer. To make the venture work successfully, employees at Johnsonville would have to make tremendous sacrifices. During the start-up phase, members would need to work six- and seven-day work weeks for months on end. Further, quality had to be maintained at the highest level to ensure that the contract continued. In the past, Stayer would have consulted with his senior management team before making a decision of this importance. This time, however, Stayer continued with his plan to revolutionize leadership practices at Johnsonville Foods. He conducted a forum with all members in the plant and presented the problem to them. Two weeks later, the members decided, almost unanimously, to take the business.

The venture was a great success. Quality rose on the new product line as well as on the original Johnsonville product line. The reject rate dropped from 5 percent to less than one-half of 1 percent. Revenues increased nineteen-fold in a ten-year period. All this occurred at a time when people were eating healthier and most other sausage products were experiencing declining sales.

Today, leadership based on trust has fully taken root at Johnsonville Foods. Members have assumed so much responsibility that Stayer has moved away from the day-to-day leadership of Johnsonville. He now works primarily on other projects, including the development of a line of pasta products and a successful consulting business. To maintain the leadership approach, every new employee attends a series of courses at "Johnsonville University," beginning with an overview of the company culture and continuing with courses in teamwork, diversity, and financial operations. The company supports a philosophy of worker involvement. Production-line employees hold meetings before each shift to discuss the operation and address any problems. Further, all members are authorized to shut down the production line at any time if they believe something isn't right. Johnsonville was recently recognized by *HR Magazine* as one of the fifty best places to work, and employees seem to agree. In an industry with turnover rates approaching 20 percent, the turnover rate at Johnsonville is a mere 8 percent.[18]

Strategy Five: Develop Core Capabilities

Know your strengths and weaknesses.

Trust in competence rests on understanding the core capabilities of an organization and working continuously to address weaknesses and get better. Strengths come from historic performance results. Competency is directly linked to hiring and retention of outstanding personnel. The commitment to continually improve, that is, get better, develops a culture of competence. Training, education, and overall organizational development all should be evaluated for their contributions to long-term trust in competence and the production of superior results. Employee needs should be regularly assessed. Goals and strategy should be directly related to core capabilities. Questions to ask include:

1. Is the organization world-class? If not, why not?
2. How should core capabilities be reflected in goals and results?
3. What needs to be strengthened?
4. What needs to fundamentally change?

Competitor assessment remains important, but focusing on internal core capabilities and describing those capabilities to stakeholders builds trust in competence.

Strategy Six: Lead Change

Generate productive change.

A leading mark of competence is the ability to identify, plan, communicate, and execute needed change. It is not a mark of competence to wait to initiate change until the organization faces a serious threat. Leaders often resist change because it is a subtle but real commentary on their current and past leadership. Recognizing the impact of a leader's resistance on others is a prerequisite to competence. More leaders can understand the need for change than can bring about productive change. It is not whether change will happen or whether crises will occur; timely response, thoughtful planning, action, and continuous communication during change and crisis are the marks of competence.

The following list provides a final series of questions leaders can use for building trust in the competence of their organization.

Questions for Building Trust in Organizational Competence
Competency and Trust in Competence

1. How can our organization assess our current competency?'

2. How can our organization assess trust in our competency?

3. Who should be responsible for these assessments?

Purpose and Vision

1. How often should we assess our purpose and vision?

2. Is our vision consistent with our core values and culture?

3. Who should be responsible for this examination?

Leadership

1. What are our greatest leadership strengths?
2. What are our greatest leadership vulnerabilities?
3. How can we better utilize our strengths and meet our challenges?
4. Who should be responsible for leadership development?

Results

1. Are we producing superior results?
2. If we are, what changes are needed to sustain performance?
3. If not, what should we do?
4. How are we communicating our results to key audiences?

Core Capabilities

1. How are we assessing our strengths?
2. How are we assessing our vulnerabilities?
3. Who is responsible for this assessment?
4. What should be done to support continuous improvement?

Change

1. What are the most likely challenges for our organization?
2. What are our greatest risks?
3. Are we engaging in regular planning to address potential change?
4. Who should lead assessment of challenges and risk?
5. Who has the responsibility for leading change?

Trust in Action: A View from Europe

In the middle of the first decade of the 21st century, Fiat was not an automobile company known for its competence. In fact, a recent *Harvard Business Review* article noted, "Four years ago, Fiat was a laughingstock."[19] Today Fiat is one of a select few automobile companies with a bottom line solidly in the black. In 2004, Sergio Marchionne became the fifth CEO in three years. He immediately identified new generations of leaders, set aggressive targets, and began benchmarking against successful companies such as Apple. The time to market for a new car was slashed from four years to a little over eighteen months. Fiat's newest car—the Cinquencento (Fiat 500)—is not only one of the smallest compacts in the world but has become the talk of the industry.

We have been closely monitoring Fiat for many years because one of the developers of our trust model, our long-time research colleague Ruggero Cesaria, is a leader in the Fiat Group Learning Service Center Corporate Programs and Advanced Learning Solutions. Cesaria has described for us business-driven leadership important for developing trust in the compe tence of any organization. Cesaria believes, "Transformational leadership is an essential condition for change and for achieving business results—both individuals and teams are needed in order to achieve such results. Leaders must have a clear business vision, challenging business objectives, execution, and a 'must' for survival. Developing leaders who can manage change is a new competency necessary for all types of organizations. Hierarchy is the past. Competent organizations of today and tomorrow are networked, boundaryless, team-based, empowered, and responsible."[20]

Cesaria described to us three components for the trustworthy, competent, and responsible organization: the market, the professions, and the informal organization. Cesaria believes the competent organization competes in its market through entrepreneurship and results-based leadership. The competent organization is populated with professionals who abide by a code of ethics, are self-regulated, cooperative, and technically skilled. Finally, the competent organization has shared values that permeate leadership and all communication exchanges. Cesaria explains, "Leaders at every level must be driven by results and aligned to core organizational values. Does the organization embrace competition and behave cooperatively? Do all organizational members know the mission, strategy, and general goals of the organization? Do they accept them? Do they know how to contribute? Are policies, rules, and actual behaviors consistent both in terms of distributive and procedural justice? Are there rich, candid, and pervasive communication patterns throughout? I have learned, at Fiat and elsewhere, that trust is not a matter of personal integrity, effort, or enthusiasm: it is embedded into social and organizational processes and cannot be left in the hands of individuals. The hierarchy, the market, and the professions used to be separate and independent worlds. But now they are sources of the new trustworthy, competent organization."

Although Cesaria was speaking about his broad experiences with competency and trust, Sergio Marchionne's description of Fiat fits Cesaria's framing of competence. Marchionne, in describing the turnaround at Fiat, said: "I had to get people energized around a clear and ambitious target. When I announced in late July 2004 that we would make two billion euros in 2007, everybody thought I was out of my mind. . . . If you set what people think is an unrealistic target, you have to help them reach it. . . . We've learned to quickly share new ideas across the organization. . . . Honoring our responsibilities to our workers is the final piece of the puzzle. A great deal of our success, I think, has come from having a committed workforce.[21]

Chapter Lessons in Trust

1. The competent organization is purpose-focused and vision-focused.

2. The competent organization has leaders who set ambitious goals, create supportive strategy and structure, expect excellence in execution, and produce results.

3. The competent organization understands its core capabilities and works to improve its weaknesses.

4. The competent organization both leads and responds to change challenges.

5. Competence and trust in competence are not the same thing.

6. Trust in competence supports positive results.

7. Distrust in competence contributes to poor results.

8. Competence building requires continuing assessment.

9. Competence building requires commitment to continual improvement.

10. Competence building is a fundamental leadership responsibility.

4

TRUST AND OPENNESS
AND HONESTY

"If you tell the truth you don't have to remember
anything."

—*Mark Twain, American author
and satirist, 1835–1910*

Integrity is the core of the open and honest organization, but
it is insufficient for an organization to be trusted. The claim
that integrity is insufficient to build trust is difficult to digest but
important to understand. The key ingredient for the open and
honest dimension of trust is that both internally and externally
people believe what they see, hear, and experience in all organizational relationships. Trust in openness and honesty always is in
the eye of the beholder. Integrity is fundamental, but the experiences of openness and honesty are the behaviors and actions
that contribute to perceptions of integrity and ultimately the
trust profile of the organization.

The Open and Honest Organization

Sarah Waller, the CEO of a small non-profit child advocacy
organization, helped us understand how important openness
and honesty were to building and maintaining trust. Sarah came
to us to assist in restructuring the organization due to its rapid
growth in case load and increase in both public and private support. Long known for her personal competence in representing
at-risk children in complex court proceedings, Sarah had convinced key community leaders of the need to expand her organization with more attorneys and to broaden services available

to children, who often were victims of serious abuse. Sarah's reputation for high integrity and competence, that is, her credibility, was strong and positive with everyone with whom we initially spoke. We were not expecting to hear from Sarah some six months after the new staff were hired and the restructuring was complete. Sarah called us because she was troubled when three of the new attorneys complained they did not have adequate information to do their jobs because Sarah controlled everything and included only a select few in decision making. The three questioned whether something was going on that was being deliberately kept from the remainder of the staff. Sarah asked us to interview her staff and work with her to determine how she should respond. What we learned illustrates the relationship between integrity and openness and honesty.

Sarah was operating no differently than she had previously. The three attorneys who had worked with her for the past ten years understood her way of working and were not troubled by the events of the past six months. All six of the new hires expressed varying degrees of discontent. The new hires claimed Sarah did not share her decisions about case loads, did not encourage the sharing of information across cases, and concealed all information about the financial operation of the organization. Three of the six new hires were convinced the organization had grown too fast and was in financial trouble. All of the new hires expressed some degree of distrust in where the organization was headed. When we provided our findings to Sarah, she quickly understood the issue. She had been taking for granted her past reputation was sufficient to help the new attorneys know they were in both an excellent and stable organization. She had not thought it necessary to explain her decisions about case assignments and believed each case should be treated individually, making sharing information across cases mostly unnecessary. She had not ever considered providing financial information, believing her attorneys would have little interest. Sarah began holding regular staff meetings at which she reviewed case loads and financial information and asked one attorney per week to brief the group on a particular current case. Sarah privately told us she thought some of these meetings were a waste of time. She did acknowledge the favorable feedback from all of the new hires and, to her surprise, the enthusiasm of her long-term employees for the explanations and discussions. Sarah's basic integrity and decision making had not changed, but she came to realize the importance of linking her core values to the communication practices of the organization. Many leaders can benefit from Sarah's experience.

As with the competence dimension of trust, the open and honest organization can be described in many different ways. We have chosen a simple description that links both research and experience. We identify an open and honest organization as one in which both internally and externally people can (1) *get the information they want and need*; (2) *get information when they want and need it*; (3) *get information in a form they can use and understand*; (4) *get information that is truthful and perceived to be truthful*; and (5) *provide information they want and need to provide*. The open and honest organization replaces a "need to know" mentality with a "need to share" approach important for trust building. A "need to know" approach tightly controls information, while a "need to share" mentality fosters information exchange important for trust. A "need to know" approach (although sometimes necessary) signals distrust by limiting access to information. A "need to share" approach signals trust by providing access and response to information whether receivers have an immediate "need" for the information or not. The "need to share" approach provides information employees need in a timely and useful manner. A "need to share" approach stimulates employees at all organizational levels to communicate information critical for problem solving, change, and innovation.

Openness and honesty contribute to perceptions of high organizational integrity, which, in turn, contributes to high organizational trust. Integrity is measured by clarity of purpose of the organization; the commitments the organization makes to employees, customers, and other stakeholders; the stated values of the organization; and organizational behaviors consistent with stated values. Although core integrity and communication practices are not the same (that is, it is possible to deliberately deceive masking breaches of integrity), integrity perceptions result from communication experiences and organizational actions.

Openness and honesty are closely linked to other dimensions of our trust model. Openness and honestly are related to others viewing an organization as reliable, as competent, as concerned for others, and as a place with which to identify. In other words, without openness and honesty, it is difficult to build high trust levels in the other dimensions important for organizational trust.

Franklin Delano Roosevelt, Joseph Stalin, and Harry Truman provide interesting examples of the openness and honesty dimension of trust. Steven Sample describes Roosevelt and Stalin: "FDR loved the American public and enjoyed their trust in return, but he misled his chief lieutenants on a daily basis. These advisers would leave a meeting convinced that FDR had a specific belief or intent, only to find he had something else entirely in mind. Working with him was not easy. Similarly, while the Soviet citizenry for the most part trusted Stalin, his own subordinates most certainly did not. Indeed, Stalin may have been one of the most untrustworthy leaders in history."[1]

Truman, who initially served as Roosevelt's vice president and became president after FDR's death, worked directly with Stalin. Truman had a completely different approach. In his biography of Truman, David McCullough describes Truman: "Ambitious by nature, he was never torn by ambition, never tried to appear as something he was not. He stood for common sense, common decency. He spoke the common tongue. As much as any president since Lincoln, he brought to the highest office the language and values of the common American people.

He held to the old guidelines: work hard, do your best, speak the truth, assume no airs, trust in God, have no fear. Yet he was not and had never been a simple, ordinary man. The homely attributes, the Missouri wit, the warmth of his friendship, the genuineness of Harry Truman, however appealing, were outweighed by the larger qualities that made him a figure of world stature, both a great and good man, and a great American president."[2]

All three of these political leaders were influential in their times and in history, but FDR, Stalin, and Truman approached openness and honesty very differently, resulting in both complex and contradictory trust profiles.

Trust in Openness and Honesty

"Honesty is the cornerstone of all success, without which confidence and ability to perform shall cease to exist."

—Mary Kay Ash, founder of Mary Kay
Cosmetics, 1915–2001

Trust in the openness and honesty of an organization contributes to tangible positive results. The economic downturn following the tragic events of September 11, 2001, was severe in both public and private sectors. Stock market losses, layoffs, slow retail sales, and increased concern for safety and security impacted all types of organizations, as well as American's personal lives. The story of how one of our clients handled a severe budget reduction illustrates what trust in openness and honesty can produce, even in the most difficult of times. A developer and manufacturer of specialized educational products for children with developmental disabilities, our client had a small but highly educated workforce who were recognized throughout the industry as leaders in adaptive technologies. Our client's leadership team was known for straightforward communication and encouragement of broad employee participation in important decision making. By December 2001, it was apparent that equipment orders had declined by 40 percent, necessitating an immediate mid-year budget rescission. The CEO of the company reacted swiftly, illustrating how important openness and honesty are in challenging circumstances. The CEO worked with his leadership team to determine the magnitude of the needed cuts and called meetings with all personnel in every section of the company to present the budget issues in great detail. At these initial meetings, he indicated ideas for budget management were welcome from all employees. He established clearly some of the choices that must be made: freezing wage increases or layoffs; freezing planned hiring or eliminating a position for each new one added; reducing all department operating budgets or more severely cutting those deemed less mission critical; and several other choices. He provided data for each alternative. The initial meetings lasted more than two hours each and closed with employees being given handouts with details and directions on how to provide input to the CEO and his leadership team. Within two weeks, employees had presented additional ideas—resulting in savings of more than $250,000. Employees expressed preferences for wage and hiring freezes over layoffs and new hires and committed to overtime without pay if orders justified. The second round of all-employee meetings presented decisions management had made to implement the cuts, explained how employee input had been utilized, and described how final decisions were made. Not a single employee left the company, and end-of-year results produced a modest profit, the only reported profit among all of the organization's competitors. Importantly, the leadership team was praised by many employees for their handling of the budget rescission process. In fact, the CEO was given a standing ovation by employees when he presented year-end results.

Our client's experience is not an isolated one. Our research and client experiences, along with the work of many others, attest to the fact that trust in openness and honesty improves the ability of an organization to collaborate, partner with others, and execute strategy on a day-to-day basis. This is not hard to understand. If I trust that you are open and honest with me, I am significantly more likely to be open and honest with you. I will share information, and that sharing contributes to enhanced creativity and innovation. Open and honest communication reduces uncertainty—I know where I stand and I know where you stand. We can engage in constructive disagreement. Reduction of uncertainty and the ability to collaborate engender more loyalty and satisfaction with all aspects of work. Accurate information is fundamental to trust building, as are explanations for decisions and a general openness and timeliness in all communication behaviors. For immediate supervisors, information flow has the strongest relationship with trust in a supervisor, including adequate explanations and timely feedback on decisions. Both managers and supervisors who freely exchange thoughts and ideas with their employees enhance overall perceptions of trust.[3] The organization is described as transparent with high trust levels.

Distrust in Openness and Honesty

"I'm not upset that you lied to me; I'm upset that from now on I can't believe you."
—Friedrich Nietzsche, German philosopher, 1844–1900

Distrust in openness and honesty produces negative outcomes. Most agree, however, that the concept of openness and honesty goes beyond simply telling the truth. It is not only truthful communication, but truth with timeliness, and in a manner that is readily accessible and understood. One of the common failings of many organizations is that the truth is provided well beyond a time when employees and external stakeholders wanted and needed the information. When information is late, distrust begins to build. When full information is not forthcoming, interpretations generated almost always become more negative and cynical than they would have been had the truth been presented earlier. What is often not understood is that individuals both within and external to the organization will not operate in an information vacuum. They will provide their own answers if the answers are not provided to them. Leaders often justify waiting to provide information until more certainty is obtained, not realizing that the interpretation of the "wait" contributes to distrust. It amazes people when we tell them it is far better in terms of trust building to say, "I don't know yet; I will get back to you as soon as I do; these are the reasons for not knowing," rather than the silence that is often characteristic at the top of the organization.

The image of Apple was tarnished in January 2009 when CEO Steve Jobs released a cryptic letter addressing concerns about his health. Jobs, a cancer survivor, explained that his sudden, and visible, weight loss was the result of a hormone imbalance. A few months later it was reported Jobs had a liver transplant. Some shareholders were not satisfied with the perceived lack of openness in the company's disclosure concerning Jobs' well-being. A loyal Apple products owner for two decades expressed his concern about the way in which the company handled the issue, "Even being a fan of Apple, I wish they would've been a little more forthright. I felt slighted. I felt disappointed."[4]

Withholding of information is seen by important stakeholders as power abuse and has been related to a host of ethical failures. Perhaps no situation in recent memory illustrates this better than the historic collapse in the financial sector that began in 2008. One stunning example of such a catastrophic trust failure was Bear Stearns. Founded in 1923, Bear Stearns was a fixture on Wall Street for eighty-five years and was rated throughout the 2000s as one of the most admired securities companies in the world by *Fortune* magazine.[5] In early March 2008, however, rumors began to circulate that Bear Stearns was experiencing dire liquidity problems. After reports that a major bank refused Bear's request for a $2 billion short-term loan to address the problem, Bear senior executives issued a press release on March 10 stating: "There is absolutely no truth to the rumors of liquidity problems that circulated today in the market." Despite this assurance, confidence continued to ebb. Bear Stearns CFO Sam Molinaro went on CNBC and claimed, the rumors were "false" adding, "There is no liquidity crisis. No margin calls. It's nonsense."[6] Bear continued to maintain publicly that all was well. On March 12, it was CEO Alan Schwartz, interviewed at a Palm Beach resort, who told CNBC, "We don't see any pressure on our liquidity, let alone a liquidity crisis."[7] As a senior executive of one competing firm put it, "To come on CNBC from Palm Beach and, you know, tell everyone everything was going to be okay, they had to be crazy."[8]

By March 13, the gravity of the company's situation had finally registered at Bear. Schwartz returned to the company's New York headquarters and convened a meeting of his top leadership to develop a strategy to deal with the rumors, but it was too late. By March 14, Bear Stearns was acquired by J.P. Morgan Chase for a mere $2 a share—a stunning price considering that Bear stock was trading at $172 a share in early 2007. In a conference call announcing the deal, Schwartz sounded as if he was still fighting reality. "Bear Stearns has been subject to a significant amount of rumor," he explained. "We attempted to try to provide some facts to the situation, but . . . the rumors intensified."[9] The collapse of Bear Stearns was complex, and many factors contributed to the unraveling of investor confidence that brought down the company. It may be an oversimplification to claim that, had the leaders at Bear Stearns been more proactive in their communication in March 2008, the company could have been saved. That said, it is clear the approach that was used by Bear executives was not successful in preventing the collapse of the eighty-five-year-old financial giant. As *Wall Street Journal* reporter Kate Kelly explains in her book,

Street Fighters: The Last 72 Hours of Bear Stearns, The Toughest Firm on Wall Street, "Once confidence in a company falls away on such a grand scale, it can never recover."[10]

In February 2009, the Texas Department of State Health Services ordered a recall of all products ever shipped from the Peanut Corporation of America plant in Plainview amid a nationwide salmonella outbreak. The order said "dead rodents, rodent excrement, and bird feathers" were discovered in a crawl space above a production area. A state inspection also found the air-handling system was pulling debris from the infested crawl space into production areas. The health department order requiring the plant to stop producing and distributing food products caused worry and confusion among consumers and store owners. More than six hundred people became ill in forty-three states, and the salmonella outbreak was linked to nine deaths. The U.S. Justice Department then conducted a criminal investigation into the manufacturing plant and the company was forced to file for bankruptcy. Shockingly, email communications between the company CEO and the plant manager indicated that, even after the Peanut Corporation learned its products were tainted with salmonella, it kept shipping them to unsuspecting customers, apparently putting profits ahead of public safety. Later, a whistle blower said he repeatedly called the unclean conditions in the production area to the attention of the company's managers, but his warnings were ignored. The impact on public trust was far-reaching, extending well beyond just the Peanut Corporation of America.[11] "They've tainted our entire industry," said Shelly Nutt, executive director of the peanut producers' board in Texas. "Public perception is killing us."[12]

It is easy to understand in our Bear Stearns and Peanut Corporation examples why withholding of information by leaders is characterized negatively. But the damage from distrust is often almost invisible. Recent research studies help us understand the subtle but important impact. Employees have been found to remain silent based on distrust of what will happen with direct openness and honesty. When employees view leadership as operating in their own self-interest, peer communication is reduced and the work environment is characterized by deliberate attempts to distort upward communication.[13]

Almost everyone reading this book can recall a time when you knew something was wrong, had a better idea, or wanted to change the way something was done but said nothing, based on the perceived lack of safety or responsiveness to new ideas or alternative viewpoints. In many ways, communication influenced by distrust is a more serious issue for trust and organizational excellence than outright lying is.

Distrust in openness and honesty results in a variety of barriers to innovation, creativity, and change. We will mention six specific barriers negatively impacting any type of organization: complacency, organizational silence, knowledge or information deficits, risk perceptions, uncertainty, and active and passive resistance.[14] Chances are you will recognize at least a version of one or more of these in your organization.

Complacency sets in when individuals within and external to the organization basically like the way things are and don't trust that communicating about the need for change is open and honest. This happens in some strange ways. Leaders may actually have communicated such positive messages about the organization (whether true or not) that no one can believe change should occur. Others become complacent because relatively low performance standards have been communicated and there is no apparent or visible crisis. Individuals and groups also deny the need for change when they are busy or stressed, have not had sufficient performance feedback, and/or do not have access to information about the entire organization.

Organizational silence is the hidden barrier because we do not observe it happening unless we engage in the behavior personally. Distrust causes individuals to remain silent in the face of issues, problems, or concerns, creating the loss of vital information necessary for making change. Leaders who do not want challenges to their authority may fail in change efforts simply because they have silenced the very information they need. When top leaders are not open, they often fear negative feedback and communicate in a manner to literally silence others who might be critical. Leaders who want to avoid embarrassment, threat, or feelings of vulnerability or incompetence may, knowingly or not, foster conditions that employees perceive as a rationale to remain silent. Several managerial beliefs about employees also contribute to this important barrier. Three are noteworthy: (1) a belief that employees are self-interested and therefore untrustworthy; (2) a belief that leaders and management know best; and (3) a belief that unity is important and dissent is to be avoided. An employee of one of our clients once told us, "It just isn't worth the risk, I feel bad, but I can't tell them they are on the wrong track. Too much is at stake. I have a family to feed." This employee was describing a major software program with which his employer was experiencing serious problems. While not revealing what the employee had told us, we strongly advised the leadership team to plan a more open and honest communication approach, increasing involvement in solving the technical problem.

Knowledge or information deficits result when distrust distances those with the most information about a problem from involvement in the solution. Closely related to organizational silence, knowledge or information deficits occur when organizations are not open to input from groups or individuals who can be expected to have critical information. In other circumstances, change occurs without leaders wanting adequate information collection. In organizations with high distrust, change may be initiated for personal gain, with little concern for the data available. One of the important aspects of this barrier is the quality of organizational participation processes. Generally speaking, broad participation throughout the organization will decrease information deficits and stimulate information exchange important for creativity, innovation, and change.

Risk perceptions are the assessments of the impact of change when the results of change are not immediately known. Risk perceptions are related to trust and distrust of those initiating the change. Risk perceptions are generally lowered when trust is high and higher when distrust is prevalent. Risk perceptions are important predictors of how committed to change employees and other stakeholders will be. As you can readily imagine, risk perceptions are related to complacency, organizational silence, and knowledge or information deficits.

Uncertainty occurs when individuals do not have enough information about how change will impact the organization and their futures. Uncertainty is related to the trust dimension of openness and honesty, because it is through communication that uncertainty can be reduced. Distrust resulting from an information vacuum or lack of trust in what is being communicated increases uncertainty. Individuals and groups create their own interpretations during uncertainty, and those interpretations usually are more negative than positive—contributing to barriers to problem solving and change.

Active and passive resistance increase when distrust is high. Active resistance includes a variety of efforts to stop a planned change. Open disagreement, voting, attempts to get others to block the change, protests, slow response to requests, and sabotage are only some of the positive and negative ways people can engage in active resistance to change. Passive resistance includes visible but not active disagreement with change: ignoring change messages and strategies, appearing to agree while not making the desired change, and a variety of other less-visible techniques. We are not suggesting that resistance should never occur. There are times when resistance to ill-conceived or ill-motivated change is very appropriate and more productive for individuals and organizations than destructive change. However, resistance, based on distrust in the openness and honesty of the organization, often blocks needed progress.

Some leaders still believe in tight control of information and basically don't support the type of environment essential for trust building. They are wrong, and we likely will not influence them to change. Many more leaders want to create and support an open and honest environment, but do not know how to do so when it must extend beyond their personal behaviors. So what can be done? Next we focus on trust building for the openness and honesty dimension of our model.

Building Trust in Openness and Honesty

"Never separate the life you live from the words you speak."

—Paul Wellstone, former Minnesota
senator and professor, 1944–2002

We are convinced that building trust in openness and honesty is based on adopting a "need to share" mentality throughout the organization, including all leaders, employees, and significant stakeholders. A "need to share" mentality is not one-way communication but a need to have processes and practices that create sharing of knowledge, ideas, issues, or problems throughout the organization and with external stakeholders. A leading proponent of this approach is Dale Meyerrose, now retired associate director of national intelligence and chief information officer, intelligence community information sharing executive. General Meyerrose first came to the "need to share" concept following the devastating events of September 11, 2001. Put in charge by the first commander of U.S. Northern Command (General Ed Eberhardt) to develop a new protocol for communicating across diverse agencies not previously connected in the development of national homeland defense, Meyerrose convened a group of his former mentors and leaders throughout government, all of whom had significant interagency experience. This group of forty individuals met in August 2002 to determine what was needed for

U.S. Northern Command to improve communication across a multiplicity of different agencies. The group focused on how to establish organizational trust and concluded "need to share" must replace "need to know" for enhanced effectiveness. Meyerrose told us, "Need to know is intended to be restrictive and a very conservative construct. There is a presumption that sharing is the last thing people should do because individuals or agencies must prove they are worthy to receive information. We stood the pyramid on its head when we adopted the 'need to share' construct."[15]

When we consider the "need to share" concept, rapidly emerging communication opportunities in social media should be considered. Over the past decade, social media such as blogs, wikis, social networking sites (SNS) like MySpace and Facebook, and the micro-blog/SNS hybrid Twitter have become an important part of organizational communication strategies. As Shel Holtz, principal of Holtz Communication + Technology, explains, "Social media is the mechanism for having a conversation and telling your story."[16] Through these media, organizational leaders and first-line workers alike can put a human face on their company. Many organizations, including IBM, Ford, Ernst & Young, Zappos.com, Southwest Airlines, Marriott Hotels, and the Transportation Safety Administration (TSA) are utilizing these media to connect with consumers. As Holtz adds, "Avoiding social media is not the answer. You cannot control the message. If you are not actively engaged, other people will tell your story for you."[17]

"Telling an organization's story" is more important than ever, as the 2009 version of the Edelman Trust Barometer reports that trust in organizations is at an all-time low, with only 38 percent of those in the United States expressing trust in business, even lower than the levels of trust in organizations reported in the wake of the Enron scandal or the dot.com collapse. At the same time, trust in "people like me" remained one of the most credible sources of information.[18] Given these realities, it is critical that organizations exhibit transparency—getting open and

honest content about the organizations out to what Holtz calls
"the edge."[19] IBM encourages its 390,000 employees to blog;
Zappos.com uses Twitter for both internal communication and as
a means for sharing the company culture with customers; Ernst
& Young uses Facebook for employee recruiting; and Southwest
Airlines (with its Nuts About Southwest website) does everything from celebrate company birthdays to deal with serious trust
issues such as the company's 2009 FAA safety violations. These
organizations and many others are working to get their content
out to the edge so their customers, partners, and even competitors can gain more insight. But what about controlling the
message? As Holtz found out when he questioned an IBM executive about the possibility of IBM employees saying something
negative about the company in blog messages, the executive
responded, "Why would we hire them if we didn't trust them?"[20]

Strategies for Building Trust in Openness and Honesty

The "need to share" approach is critical for trust in openness and
honesty. But before we describe specific strategies in support of
the "need to share" concept, we want to re-state the foundational
nature of integrity. We value core integrity; it is the base of the
high-trust organization. However, we hope we have convinced
you that having integrity and others believing the organization
has integrity are not the same things. Our strategies are designed
to ensure communication processes and practices to support core
integrity and build trust. The strategies we present should never
be used to mask deceit or promote power and ethical abuses.

Strategy One: Assess Openness and Honesty and Trust in Openness and Honesty

*Conduct a complete and thoughtful assessment of the current
state of openness and honesty throughout the organization and the*

extent to which stakeholders trust the openness and honesty of the organization.

The assessment requires assigning specific responsibility and accountability for its completion, asking key questions, and committing to listen and act on the answers. Key questions include:

1. What department and which individuals have the expertise to design a comprehensive assessment? What are the resources needed to support assessment work?

2. Does the organization's culture support openness and honesty or more controlled information? Do the core values of the organization support a "need to share" perspective?

3. Can you identify areas of distrust in openness and honesty? What can you learn from these examples?

4. Can you identify areas of trust in openness and honesty? What can you learn from these examples?

5. Who will assume responsibility for responding to the assessment?

Strategy Two: Assess Communication Practices

Conduct a comprehensive assessment of communication practices.

Communication practices vary widely across organizations. What we are recommending is organization-specific. The recommended assessment relates to all regularly occurring communication events and practices, ranging from staff meetings to performance evaluation. It includes internal and external communication departments and stockholder and regulatory relationships. The assessment assists the organization in understanding the type of information control or sharing that is regularly occurring. The assessment includes a comprehensive review of various media including social networking. The regular practices of an organization reflect what the organization values and are critical to understanding both trust and distrust in openness and honesty. If desired, this assessment can be combined with Strategy

One. However, they are different, and the distinctiveness of each should not be compromised in a combination of efforts. Strategy One is about assessing the core openness and honesty and trust in openness and honesty of the organization. Strategy Two is identifying the regular communication practices throughout the organization and with its stakeholders in order to determine how these events and practices can contribute to trust building.

Strategy Three: Assess Leadership

Excel at leadership communication.

Take a focused look at the communication capabilities of senior leaders. What are the expectations for high integrity, openness, and honesty? Is there trust among the senior leadership team? If not, what should be done? Does the senior leadership team constructively challenge each other and seek input from throughout the organization? If not, what should be done? Does senior leadership listen, really listen? Steven Sample describes a particularly useful approach. Sample suggests, "The value of thinking gray—taking in information and suspending judgment with respect to its truth or falsity as long as possible. An important part of thinking gray for a leader is *listening* gray—absorbing stories, reports, complaints, posturings, accusations, extravagant claims, and prejudices without immediately offering a definitive response."[21] Excelling at leadership communication requires commitment and accountability beginning at the very top. Top leaders set the tone for the communication practices of the entire organization. An organization will not benefit from high trust in openness and honesty without the commitment and involvement of its leadership team.

Strategy Four: Develop Core Communication Capabilities

Continually develop the core capabilities of those involved with significant communication responsibilities.

In Strategy Three we focused on top leaders, and they are not excluded from this strategy of continuous improvement. However, Strategy Four focuses on front-line responsibilities of supervisors, information technology personnel, team members, and specific internal and external communication departments.

What are the communication expectations for supervisors? Is their performance evaluated in part on their openness and honesty? Do they have the skills to run effective meetings? Do they provide excellent performance feedback to employees? Do they listen, really listen? Do IT personnel understand important distinctions between technical connectivity and effective communication? Do IT professionals make technical recommendations that support excellent human communication? Are the internal and external communication departments effective and prepared to contribute to trust building? What expertise do professionals have with emerging communications technologies and social media? What about training? Communication competencies appropriate for trust building cannot be assumed, even with highly educated people. Building trust in openness and honesty requires work and a thoughtful understanding throughout the organization that effective and ethical communication is a broadly shared responsibility.

Strategy Five: Develop the Communication Plan

Create a compelling, comprehensive communication plan.

Far too many organizations think communication planning only involves efforts by communication professionals to develop internal and external messages. A compelling, comprehensive communication plan includes members throughout the organization and does not leave to chance addressing important issues, problems, successes, or needs for change.

The communication plan begins with identifying and clarifying the values for openness and honesty the organization can support. To increase trust, these values must be real and must be reflected in communication policies, processes, and practices. An underlying assumption is that the plan will permit the intentional framing of messages to reflect the integrity of the organization and increase its openness and honesty profile. It is not our purpose to specify what an individual organization should value, but there are several general values that research and experience have related to high-trust organizations. Specifically, openness and honesty are more likely to be trusted when the organization values straight talk and the truth and confronts reality. When organizations demonstrate respect through individual behaviors and their policies and practices, they are more highly evaluated along trust dimensions. Giving credit where credit is due is linked to respect and openness and honesty. Finally, organizations which listen and handle problems at the lowest possible levels receive higher marks for trustworthiness than organizations which primarily focus on top leaders for solution generation and implementation.

Once values and expectations for communication responsibilities have been clarified, the plan moves to the specifics of (1) identifying themes and other types of information that need to be communicated and by whom; (2) identifying audiences that should regularly receive information; (3) identifying audiences that should regularly provide information; (4) describing types of media to be utilized; (5) assessing timing and frequency of various types of communication practices; (6) assessing how the plan supports the development of relationships; and (7) determining how the plan should be continually evaluated. Identifying who is accountable for plan development and implementation is important, but the final responsibility rests with top leaders.

We return to our interview with Angelique Rewers, president and owner of Bon Mot Communications, when she talked with us about the important role of corporate communicators in building trust and her belief that not many organizations make a conscious effort to build trust. She contended corporate communicators need to take the lead in working with leadership to understand trust building. Rewers explained, "Trust is a communications issue. We establish trust with others through our interactions with them and, over time, as commitments are made and kept and words and actions are seen to be genuine, individuals come to trust." She specifically identified tactical recommendations she has made in both a white paper and also on her e-zine, *The Corporate Communicator*, which frequently covers the issue of trust.[22]

"*Start a dialogue about trust with your executive team.* An organizational trust campaign must have buy in from the highest levels.

"*Define a distinctive organizational mission.* An organization that wants to establish trust with its stakeholders must start with a grounded sense of what defines it—why it exists, what it stands for, and what differentiates it in the marketplace of customers, investors, and workers.[23]

"*Complete a trust-focused communications audit.* Take a look back at all communications with each key stakeholder group over the last six months. Include press releases, advertisements, executive communiqués, web and blog postings (internal and external), newsletters, town hall transcripts, and so on. Then evaluate those communications for their openness and honesty. Look at whether or not any commitments were made in those communications— and if those commitments were kept. Finally, determine if there was consistency in messaging across each platform.

"*Conduct a trust-based risk assessment.* When it comes to trust, it's much more difficult to rebuild it than it is to maintain it. That is why it is so important to be proactive. Start by looking across your organization and pinpointing all of the touch points with your key stakeholder groups. Then identify the areas that are either most vulnerable to a breach of trust or that would cause the most damage to your reputation if there was a breach of trust. For example, an organization has hundreds of customer service representatives taking calls twenty-four hours per day faces the risk that any one of those representatives could breach a customer's trust at any moment.

"Once the highest threats for a potential breach of trust are identified, you need to develop a risk mitigation plan. In the customer service example, you might offer additional training to customer service representatives, including an overview on how social media tools like YouTube and MySpace are making it all the more important to provide excellent service on each and every call.

"*Create SOPs for major risks.* Even with a risk-mitigation plan, you still need to be prepared for the inevitable breach of trust. How quickly and effectively your organization responds can make all the difference in whether the hit to your reputation is a mere chip in the armor or a devastating blow. By creating standard operating procedures (SOPs) for various scenarios ahead of time, your organization will be able to recover quickly in the event of a trust crisis.

"*Bust through the bureaucracy.* It is increasingly difficult today for organizations to maintain traditional command-and-control systems. Employees no longer accept old-fashioned hierarchical cultures and management approaches. They don't want to know simply what it is they are supposed to do; they want to know why they are supposed to do it and how that contributes to the organization's overall success. Communications (and the policies and programs they describe) should reflect this increased demand for openness.

"*Start sharing more information.* CHA, a U.K.-based consultancy, found that 90 percent of employees who are kept fully informed are motivated to deliver added value by staying with a company longer and working harder, while 80 percent of those who are kept in the dark are not. In addition, organizations with effective communication are 4.5 times more likely to report high levels of employee engagement, and companies with high levels of communication effectiveness are 20 percent more likely to report lower turnover rates than their competitors.[24] As communicators, it is our job to encourage executives to share information more frequently and more openly.

"*Train on trust.* Managers should take advantage of training workshops and toolkits to understand how to communicate to build trust. In addition, organizations must hold managers accountable by incorporating communication and trust-related metrics into performance evaluations. These measures can be tracked through employee engagement surveys and 360-degree feedback loops.

"*Promote corporation responsibility.* If your organization is looking to build trust among Generations X and Y, it will need to behave in a socially responsible manner. When asked what makes them trust a company, younger opinion elites place more importance on a company's social and environmental track records than on its financial performance and say it is much more important for a company seeking to build its reputation to practice sound environmental policies than it is to simply make charitable contributions. With that said, corporate communicators must be sure that their organizations' environmental and community efforts are of genuine intentions and [not] merely a ploy for 'good PR.'"

Several of our clients have incorporated comprehensive communication planning into their strategic planning. As Rewers suggests, auditing communication for trust is essential for planning. Many of our clients have coupled strategic plan development with assessment of organizational trust, using the trust profile described later in Chapter Nine and included on a CD at the back of this book. Our clients have seen statistically significant increases in their positive trust profiles by developing and executing excellent communication plans.

The list below provides questions leaders can ask for building trust in openness and honesty.

Questions for Building Trust in Organizational Openness and Honesty
Assessment of Openness and Honesty and Trust

1. How can our organization assess our current openness and honesty?

2. How can our organization assess the trust stakeholders have in our openness and honesty?

3. Who should be responsible for these assessments?

Communication Practices

1. How effective are our communication practices in supporting openness and honesty?

2. What are our strengths in communication practices?

3. What are our challenges in communication practices?

4. What should change to improve performance?

5. Who should be responsible for improvements?

Leadership Communication

1. What are our greatest leadership communication strengths?

2. What are our greatest leadership communication vulnerabilities?

3. How can we better utilize our strengths and meet our challenges?

4. Who should be responsible for leadership development?

Core Communication Competencies

1. Do organizational members at all levels have clear communication expectations and accountabilities?

2. Does training support continual development of communication capabilities?

3. Are internal and external communication departments developing strategies to support a high-trust profile?

4. Who should be responsible for competency development?

Communication Planning

1. Are organizational values supportive of integrity and openness and honesty?

2. What should our organizational communication plan incorporate?

3. Who should be involved in organizational communication planning?

4. What messages should we develop?

5. Where do we need feedback?

6. What media should be utilized?

7. How should we evaluate our efforts?

8. Who is responsible for communication planning and evaluation?

Trust in Action: The Intelligence Community Story

Few associate trust building through information sharing with the intelligence community. The events of this decade provide an interesting shift in practice and strategy. On February 22, 2008, an almost unprecedented publication was issued by J.M. McConnell, director of national intelligence, and Dale Meyerrose, associate director of national intelligence and chief information officer, intelligence community information sharing executive. The *United States Intelligence Community Information Sharing Strategy* was published with a somewhat revolutionary opening statement: "The need to share information became an imperative to protect our Nation in the aftermath of the 9/11 attacks on our homeland. The Intelligence Community's 'need-to-know' culture, a necessity during the Cold War, is now a handicap that threatens our ability to uncover, respond, and protect against terrorism and other asymmetric threats. . . . A central principle is the recognition that information sharing is a behavior and not a technology."[25] We interviewed General Meyerrose in October 2008, six years after he began working with the "need to share" concept, first at U.S. Northern Command and then as the nation's first Intelligence Community Information Sharing Executive. Meyerrose told us, "In the past six years, I have refined my thinking a lot. We have just published the first information-sharing strategy for the U.S. government. It is about changing processes and mindsets in organizations to realize their success is contingent on their linkages with other organizations."

Meyerrose described for us major lessons about information sharing from his U.S. Northern Command days to becoming the first-ever Intelligence Community Information Sharing Executive (a Presidential appointment requiring U.S. Congressional confirmation):

> "Think big, start small, scale fast. I believe this to be the 'organizational leadership Holy Grail' in both entrepreneurial and bureaucratic endeavors. Thinking big is the compass, vision, goal, or desired outcome for all participants. Start small connotes making the issue real, provides an understandable platform to start working together, and allows everyone the opportunity to develop trust in the 'thinking big proposition.' Scale fast becomes the strategy to outcomes (the think big part) based on the lessons learned and trust developed during the early execution (the start small part). The wisdom and leadership come in knowing how big, how small, and how fast, given the task and developing interaction among the stakeholders.

> "The underlying premise of 'need to share' or 'responsibility to provide' paradigms shifts the 'burden of trust' in organizational

relationships from the entities that potentially need shared information to those who have the information. In a 'need to know' culture, organizations desiring information have to prove themselves worthy to receive same. A 'need to share' philosophy assumes that potential receiving organizations are worthy, unless proven to the contrary. Many wrongly presume that 'need to share' means an indiscriminate and frivolous release of information that needs protection. But where one puts the 'burden of trust' is the difference between an environment as open as possible versus one that is as closed as possible.

"The 'need to share' acknowledges that organizational success is linked to sharing with others. No organization is totally self-sufficient—particularly in government. Finding and leveraging this motivation is the fuel for information sharing. It is almost like the business of information sharing is knowledge development and growth. Parts of the U.S. government are hidebound, process oriented to the point process controls everything. Only after they come out with the wrong outcomes do they go back. Getting people to focus on the outcomes, not the purity of the inputs, is critical.

"The 'need to share' too often invokes the thought of sharing data or finished product. While there is merit to this perspective, the real power of information sharing leads to developing knowledge. Thus, the need for collaboration might be the real goal, rather than 'I'll show you my stuff, if you show me your stuff.' Subject-matter experts from various organizations, working through/within a trusted exchange environment and sharing the process of problem solving as well as data and information, produce a higher quality of knowledge and understanding. The business of information sharing is knowledge development and growth.

"Understand that there are various desired purposes for information sharing: shared situation awareness, collaboration, decision making, and event management. The focus of many information-sharing issues becomes information technology—making systems/networks/data bases interoperable. IT is the input of the equation, and largely performs as designed. Information sharing is an outcome-base proposition. When you develop a culture of information sharing, IT personnel design systems/networks/databases that support the desired outcome of sharing and collaboration. So policies that deal with 'write for release," digital rights management, identity, and information handling are far more powerful than working IT system connections.

"How can you lower what you don't know? Trust is huge. Trust is built on success, little actions, so you and I can be on the same team and it can be a good thing."[26]

Chapter Lessons in Trust

1. Integrity is the core of the open and honest organization.

2. Integrity is insufficient for high trust in organizational openness and honesty.

3. An open and honest organization exhibits "need to share" values.

4. Trust in openness and honesty contributes to tangible positive outcomes.

5. Distrust in openness and honesty contributes to negative outcomes.

6. Distrust contributes to withholding of information and power and ethical abuses.

7. Distrust contributes to barriers to innovation, creativity, and change.

8. Building trust in openness and honesty begins with assessment of openness and honesty and the trust stakeholders have in openness and honesty.

9. Leaders and all organizational members should continually develop communication capabilities.

10. Top leaders set the standard for organizational integrity, openness, and honesty alignment.

5

TRUST AND CONCERN FOR STAKEHOLDERS

"Whatever we accomplish is due to the combined effort. The organization must be with you or you don't get it done. In my organization there is respect for every individual, and we all have a keen respect for the public."

—*Walt Disney, artist, Hollywood entertainer, and the creator of Disney theme parks, 1901–1966*

Genuine caring for employees, customers, and other stakeholders characterizes organizations that are evaluated highly in the concern dimension of our trust model. Concern for stakeholders is exhibited in a host of communication exchanges, as well as in virtually all organizational policies and practices. Trust in concern for stakeholders is directly related to employee and customer loyalty. Poor Richard's is one of the best examples we know of a locally owned restaurant that has not only survived but thrived for more than thirty years against major chain competition. Poor Richard's success is in large measure due to demonstrated care for both employees and customers.

The Concerned for Stakeholders Organization

Poor Richard's includes a restaurant, café and wine bar, bookstore, and toy store, employing forty-five dedicated and committed staff. In an interview with owners Richard Skorman and Patricia Seator, who describe themselves as "life and business partners," it became evident genuine concern for others is fundamental to their business model. They allocate 40 percent of gross sales to employee benefits, twice as much as most other restaurants. Their benefits include paying a living wage at all levels of employment, participation in a profit-sharing plan that encourages staff commitment to success, a full health plan with dental care, and paid vacations for all staff from dishwashers to managers. A loan policy allows any employee to borrow up to $50 with only the approval of his or her direct supervisor. Repayment comes out of the employee's paycheck. Larger loans require the approval of the two owners, who say they "have only been badly burned one time." Richard co-signed on a $5,000 loan so an employee could start a carpet cleaning company. When the cleaning company failed, Richard had to pay the loan. Despite this experience, Skorman and Seator continue to support their employees and those at Poor Richard's are inspired by the owners' concern for them.

Other stories recounted by Richard and Patricia demonstrate a similar concern for their customers. During a national scare concerning peanut butter contaminated with salmonella, Richard asked his cooking staff to stop using peanut butter prior to any official recalls. He took this action without concern for potential cost because it was the right thing to do for his customers. The message was clear. The employees at Poor Richard's realized the restaurant owners care as much about customers and their well-being as about themselves and the staff. On another occasion, a group of customers observed a thief grabbing a purse and running out of the restaurant. The customers ran after the thief, confronted him in a parking lot, and returned the purse to the restaurant. Richard and Patricia believe caring for others is characteristic of those who dine at Poor Richard's.[1]

Research and our experience with other clients support what we learned from Skorman and Seator. The organization that is concerned for stakeholders communicates respect, provides encouragement and support, and works to change wrongs.

The concerned organization aligns policies and practices with a genuine attitude of caring for employees, customers, clients, vendors, investors, or donors. Top management is responsible for communicating a culture of caring and supporting policies and practices, which exhibit caring. Individuals at all organizational levels are engaged in exhibiting concern for others, are empowered to take action to challenge wrongs, and generally adopt an attitude of supporting the welfare of employees, customers, clients, vendors, and investors or donors. Organizations evaluated highly on the concern trust dimension have top leaders and immediate supervisors communicating regularly about the well being of employees. Supervisors, in particular, communicate support for the personal well-being of those who report to them. Of equal importance, highly trusted organizations listen—really listen—to employees, customers, clients, vendors, investors, or donors. Organizational policies and practices communicate fairness and support to employees and customers. Hiring, performance appraisal, leave policies, wages, grievance and disciplinary processes, and promotional practices all contribute to whether employees believe the organization is concerned for them. Opportunities for personal growth and development are directly linked to employees' trust in that concern.

When we began to develop our trust model, we focused on concern for employees. Over the past decade, we have expanded our work to include diverse stakeholders. We have learned customers or clients evaluate concern based on service support, pricing, product or service quality, dispute-resolution policies, timeliness, and overall ease and accessibility of interacting with the organization. Organizations having confidence in the abilities of stakeholders and recognizing stakeholder contributions are more likely to be evaluated highly in the concern for stakeholders' dimension. The highly trusted organization is seen as fair and caring about justice in relationships and transactions. The goal of the concerned organization is the well-being of all stakeholders based on fairness and justice.

Trust in Concern for Stakeholders

"One of the hardest things in the world is to admit
you are wrong. And nothing is more helpful in
resolving a situation than its frank admission."
—Benjamin Disraeli, British prime minister, 1804–1881

Trust in concern for stakeholders is directly related to employee satisfaction and perceptions of overall organizational effectiveness. Employees are retained at a higher rate when they trust their organizations are concerned for their welfare. Importantly, employees are more productive when they believe they are working in an organization that cares about their well-being. Customers are more loyal to organizations that care about their needs, whether for quality products and services or for timely response to problems. Stephen M.R. Covey refers to genuine caring as a motive, which inspires trust when coupled with an agenda of mutual benefit.[2] We believe Covey's description of mutual benefit is fundamental for the concern and caring, which support superior organizational results. When an organization exhibits concern and caring for stakeholders, stakeholders are more likely to trust the organization, to be loyal and productive, and to care about what happens to the organization.

The experience of a major U.S. call center illustrates the importance of concern for stakeholders. Part of a large pharmaceutical corporation, the call center was instrumental in taking orders and creating shipments for drugs throughout North America. The company regularly conducted extensive industry benchmarking. Leaders were convinced their call center costs were too high and customers were not as satisfied with either responsiveness or accuracy of telephone and electronic transactions. The center handled approximately ten thousand orders daily, with thirty employees each taking approximately twenty calls per hour and another twenty employees processing orders submitted electronically. Accuracy rates exceeded 90 percent; however, leaders believed the rate should range slightly above 98 percent. Customer surveys rated the center above average, and orders had increased each of the last three years. We were asked to interview the leadership team, review benchmarking and center data, and talk with employees about their perceptions of their own effectiveness. What we learned was interesting and important. The leadership team daily reviewed data and identified employees who were taking the most calls and electronic transactions. Monthly, they reviewed error reports and customer complaints. The leadership team produced a chart of all employees ranked from highest to lowest in productivity, that is, numbers of transactions processed and accuracy rates combined. Individuals were provided with their own statistics monthly, and a chart without names was posted at all work stations. Merit raises were given only to those who were in the top 25 percent on the productivity chart for eight months out of a twelve-month period. Our review of the benchmarking and center data indicated the center was processing transactions slightly above their competitors, but error rates were indeed 2 to 5 percentage points higher per one thousand transactions. When we talked with employees, another picture readily became apparent. Employees believed all management cared about was the numbers. The "chart," as it was known, did not take into account anything that happened in an employee's life and made it very difficult for most to qualify for merit raises. Only twelve out of all fifty employees had received merit increases the previous year. (All employees received a cost-of-living increase based on inflation.) We were told four employees had had deaths in their immediate families and two others had experienced serious illness. When these employees returned to work, they told us they had trouble staying with the pace and had experienced error increases. They believed management did not care about their personal stresses.

We asked what the employees believed contributed to an error rate that exceeded their competitors' rate. Several senior employees told us it was the absolute pressure to produce daily transaction numbers. They stressed they could not help less-experienced members of their group because their personal numbers would go down. Two of the highest performers on the "chart" said training was not adequate, and they were not encouraged to assist with troubleshooting problems. We asked the employees what could be done. Several employees told us about one of their principal competitors, where the call center was organized in self-managing teams with results based on overall team versus individual performance. They indicated this company had the lowest error rates in the industry and was on a par in daily transactions processed with industry leaders. We asked if that information had been provided to the leadership team. The answer was a resounding "no." One employee said, "They don't trust us, don't care about us as anything but numbers. We could fix this problem in a hurry if we were given the opportunity."

When we talked with the leadership team, they were shocked and dismayed. The division manager said, "I get it, I really get it. We have been so focused on numbers—they are important for sure—but we missed the big picture. I actually do care about these people, but they are making more money with us than they can anywhere else in this state. I never realized they might think they are only a statistic. I can sure understand how the error rate is where it is. We stopped extensive training about five years ago. We just assumed there was enough time to deal with these issues and meet the numbers."

Over the next several months, the leadership team and senior employees explored the concept of self-management used by two of their competitors and visited call centers using self-management structures in other industries. They worked with us to develop a change plan that would move the center from individual metrics to team metrics. They presented benchmarking data to employees and asked for their input on solving the errors problems. Training for self-managing teams was provided for leaders and employees. The leadership team selected the composition of the teams and asked each team to set goals for the metrics they would produce. The division manager publicly told employees he regretted the perception that their well-being was not important to the organization. He acknowledged how the "chart" had contributed to this perception. He stressed metrics remained important but said teams would have the responsibility for posting their own results. Teams would work with other teams to ensure high productivity was maintained and errors lowered. Teams were permitted to contribute to the design of their work areas and determine how work would be distributed. Most teams changed previous work assignments to have members work with both the phones and electronic orders. Senior team members were designated as "problem solvers," with the knowledge that their individual metrics might be reduced on a given day when they stepped in to solve problems designed to lower error rates. The overall budget for the merit pool was not increased. Awards no longer went to individuals, but to teams. For a few employees, the amount of their merit increases actually decreased because the money now was spread across all team members. At the end of the first year of team-based operations, transactions processed per day remained stable and the error rate improved to less than 2 percent per one thousand transactions. Importantly, employees told us management now listened to them. The most senior employees believed employees were more committed to high performance because they were no longer treated as numbers. More performance data were posted by the teams than had been posted on the dreaded "chart." The leadership team was more than pleased. The division manager told us he was not convinced employees trusted management really cared about them, but he thought they were moving in the right direction. We agreed. This is an excellent example of an organization designed for mutual benefit—employees were listened to for their ideas, empowered to make change, and rewarded for their efforts. Management changed its approach to getting results and became more employee-centered. Results improved, demonstrating the viability of thinking broadly about trusting employees. Although not part of our work and impossible for us to measure, the decrease in errors also benefited customers, undoubtedly contributing to their trust in the organization's performance.

Distrust in Concern for Stakeholders

"In low trust cultures, we hide our failures, we protect ourselves not others."

—*Anonymous Spanish computer scientist*

Leigh Branham, owner of Keeping the People Inc., interpreted data from over nineteen thousand exit interviews and his own employee surveys. His research findings suggest a lack of trust in senior leaders is the number-one reason people leave organizations.[3] Branham's work challenges the popular belief that money is the most common reason why employees leave their jobs—he claims it is trust.

Branham contends, "The sense of loyalty is pretty much gone . . . workers leave because of pushes—not because they were pulled away by better job offers." We agree. Work with our clients and our trust research provide evidence employees feel pushed to leave an organization where their individual needs cannot be met or where they feel they simply are not valued. Employees do not trust organizations are concerned for them when leaders talk about employees as overhead, labor costs, and resources. Employees trust organizations in which leaders describe them as assets, competitive advantage, and critical to achievement of goals. Employee downsizing over the last decade has eroded employee trust in concern, even among organizations known for employee loyalty.

Executive compensation packages have been evaluated by employees as a measure of how organizational leaders do or do not value employee contributions. A member of our team, Michael Hackman, and his colleague Craig Johnson have looked at this issue for a number of years. They report, "Corporate executives in the United States often live like royalty; they are the highest paid in the world and enjoy such perks as chauffeur driven limousines, private jets, and executive dining rooms."[4] Between 1990 and 2007, the average pay for the chief executives of S&P 500 companies quadrupled to $10.5 million (including salary, bonus, stocks, and stock option grants). This figure is 344 times the pay of the typical American worker, whose salary barely kept pace with inflation during the same period.[5] Huge compensation packages exist side-by-side with reduction in numbers of jobs in many organizations. While justifications for these differences can be argued, the lowering of employee trust has produced negative consequences. Soaring compensation packages might be justified if there were a consistent correlation between CEO pay and performance. There isn't. To make matters worse, some failed executives have been richly rewarded. Fired Pfizer CEO Henry McKinnell received $83 million in pension benefits, even though Pfizer stock declined nearly 37 percent during his tenure. Former Home Depot and current Chrysler CEO Bob Nardelli walked away from Home Depot with a $210 million severance package despite the fact that the company's share price remained flat during his six years on the job.[6] And although the disparity in compensation levels between the boardroom and the shop floor exists in other countries, U.S. chief executives have a clear lead with the highest pay packages among their counterparts in other advanced countries.[7] All of this seems to be negatively impacting trust as a 2008 Gallup/USA Today poll reported 63 percent of Americans felt that it was very important to set limits on executive compensation as a part of the government's efforts to deal with the financial problems on Wall Street.[8] Indeed, this perception may have impacted President Obama in 2009 when he imposed a $500,000-a-year pay cap for executives receiving tax-payer bailout funds. Distrust also fueled the furor over the AIG bonuses in March 2009.

Training and development programs are seen by employees as practices with the potential to be positive expressions of concern for employee development. The same programs, however, can carry negative messages about the importance of specific individuals or groups of employees. The issues are straightforward: (1) How are employees selected for training programs? (2) Are the programs a prerequisite to promotional opportunities? (3) Are training programs and budgets adequate for employee needs? and (4) Do training programs meet management needs? Often organizations do not understand how cuts in training budgets may be perceived by employees as generating limitations on advancement opportunities. Increasingly, organizations are asking employees to seek development opportunities external to the organization. Questions immediately surface about: (1) Who has access to external programs? (2) Is there tuition assistance? (3) Are work schedules conducive to educational opportunities? and (4) How does the organization assist in identifying programs that are most likely to contribute to development. The key for these types of programs is a belief in the fairness of employee selection for participation and the linking of programs to both employee and organizational needs. Programs that employees believe are fair and equitable contribute to trust, while perceptions of favoritism or exclusive access to development opportunities contribute to distrust in concern for employees.

Several organizational processes are central to trust or distrust in concern for employees: hiring, performance evaluation, merit pay, promotional practices, and grievance and conflict resolution policies and practices. Fair treatment is at the core of trust and distrust. Fair treatment supports trust in concern, and perceptions of unfair treatment generate distrust. It is that simple. Distrust grows when employees believe the most competent person was not hired, promoted, given a good performance evaluation, or did not receive a merit increase. Distrust grows when employees believe the grievance process is stacked against them and protects management. Distrust grows when the conflict resolution process takes too long, contributing to heightened conflict. When distrust grows, loyalty decreases, resulting in both retention problems and, at a minimum, the lowering of productive efforts.

The trust relationships an organization experiences with its customers or clients are based in part on how concern for customers and clients is exhibited by the organization. Product and service quality contribute to customer and client evaluations of trust and are predictive of whether customers or clients remain loyal. Access to organizational assistance and quality of problem resolution contribute to trust or distrust. Pricing strategies, product return policies, financing programs, and a host of other customer policies contribute to whether there is trust or distrust in an organization. As with employee trust, most of the trust evaluations from customers or clients are based on whether they have been treated fairly by the organization and with concern for their well-being.

We provide a sad example from a technology start-up company wherein management believed certain new product features had been leaked to an important competitor. We talked with the CEO of this company following the resignation of three of their most capable design engineers. The CEO was distraught because he perceived the loss of these talented engineers compromised the company's ability to meet the deadlines that were so important for their new product introduction. The CEO wanted to beat any competitors at introducing the new technology and had been on track for a successful launch prior to the reported leaks and resignations. We asked about the leaks. The CEO said it was impossible to determine for sure whether the leaks had occurred, but his marketing manager had learned from two potential clients about a competitor describing new product features possible only with what the CEO believed was their proprietary technology. When pressed for details, both customers had become evasive. We asked what the CEO and his team had done to determine whether there were leaks. He responded he had done something he never would have believed he would have to do. He asked his human resources and security departments to review email accounts for all design engineers and for those with prototype responsibilities in manufacturing. He also had security review the email records for his marketing employees, including the marketing manager. Additionally, he asked his security personnel to install recording devices on selected telephones. We then asked him about the reaction to such measures, he paused and then told us what happened. Our CEO had revealed to his leadership team the extent of his investigation. Two members of the team were livid, although the company's legal counsel indicated no laws had been broken. He also told the team he had found two or three suspicious emails, but not enough to define specifically whether the individuals in question had been responsible for the assumed leaks. The CEO contended no employees knew about the investigations. We doubted his assessment of the situation. We asked to interview individually members of the leadership team and the engineers who had resigned. Leadership team members privately expressed to us they considered the CEO's actions a breach of trust in them and in their highly competent employees. They agreed something should have been done, but would have chosen a much more direct process. Two of the three engineers who resigned agreed to talk with us. Both of these individuals strongly expressed the belief they could no longer work for an organization where they were not trusted. They did not challenge the CEO's right to investigate, but believed his tactics expressed no confidence in them or concern for how they would react to such surveillance. We asked how they knew about the email searches and phone recordings. Both indicated members of the leadership team had talked with them following the meeting when the CEO disclosed his tactics.

You may wonder why we think this example is indicative of distrust in concern for employees and not an example of openness and honesty. Obviously, this is about openness, although not about honesty. We believe this example is important for the concern dimension of trust because what was in question was the lack of respect and lack of trust the CEO's approaches to investigating the problem evidenced. Both leadership team members and the engineers in question agreed the CEO had the need to investigate and the authority to do so; and the leadership team believed he gave them an honest account of his findings. What they did not believe was that the CEO trusted them or respected them because of the methods he used to try to understand the problem. He inadvertently violated the basics of exhibiting concern for others, that is, respecting and trusting them. The results for the company were devastating. The product release was delayed for four months. An important member of the leadership team followed the engineers to another company. A principal competitor introduced a similar product two weeks prior to the delayed product launch. The CEO worked hard to explain to both his leadership team and to all employees that he had made a mistake in judgment, although not in intent. He stated he did trust his workforce and wanted them to stay. The late product launch reduced the profitability of what had been planned as a major new release. It was never learned whether the competitor who launched the similar product had access to information from within the company. Although the company survived, the CEO and others agreed significant trust had been eroded, requiring long-term work to repair.

Contrast this example with the 2006 episode between corporate rivals Coca-Cola and PepsiCo and you see that trust can be built, even when there are competing interests at stake. In May 2006, executives at Pepsi's corporate headquarters in Purchase, New York, received a letter from someone claiming to be a high-level Coca-Cola employee offering to sell details and confidential information regarding Coke's secret formula and new product development. Pepsi officials immediately notified executives at Coca-Cola, who then contacted the FBI. The resulting sting operation led to the arrest of an executive assistant who worked at Coca-Cola headquarters in Atlanta, Georgia, and her two accomplices. The three were arrested on the day they planned to exchange the sensitive information with an FBI operative for $1.5 million. As U.S. Attorney David Nahmias explained, "Some of this information is as important to the Coca-Cola Company as classified information is to the government."[9] As a Pepsi executive noted, the company did what any responsible organization would do and that "competition can sometimes be fierce, but must always be fair and legal."[10]

In a fundamental way, concern for what is right always includes a concern for the impact of actions on others. Trust that an organization has concern for its stakeholders begins with a basic evaluation of what is right and what impact an action has on all involved. Next we will identify strategies for building trust in concern.

Building Trust in Concern for Stakeholders

> "Respect is not trust. Trust has to be earned through
> courageous conduct and demonstrated character.
> Character is sustained courage. We can respect
> everyone, but we can't trust everyone."
> —Gus Lee, *author and motivational speaker*

Building trust in concern for stakeholders is based on a genuine caring for others, a commitment to doing what is right, and a belief that caring and commitment will generate organizational excellence. However, building trust in concern is more than leadership intent. It is the continual examination of communication, policies, practices, and processes for the concern and caring they reflect. It is aligning intent with action and developing an understanding of how stakeholders evaluate the impact of action.

Strategies for Building Trust in Concern for Stakeholders

"We always wanted the very best for our members. It was important they know we set our goals with their needs and well-being in mind."

—*Anonymous non-profit leader*

The trust-building strategies we present are designed to help organizations align intent, behavior, policies, and practices. While not the only strategies an organization can or should employ, they represent an important first step in building trust in concern.

Strategy One: Assess Concern for Stakeholders and Trust in Concern for Stakeholder

Conduct a complete and thoughtful assessment of the current state of concern for stakeholders throughout the organization and the extent to which stakeholders trust the organization's concern for them.

By now you are seeing a pattern in our strategies. We begin with assessment and then move to action for trust building. We do not support random action without a thoughtful understanding of the current state of trust. We see much too much random action followed by disappointment when results are minimal at best. As with the other assessments, we are recommending (and these assessments can be combined into one effort if desired), specific responsibility and accountability for assessment completion should be identified. Key questions should be developed with a commitment to listen and act on the answers. Key questions include:

1. What department and which individuals have the expertise to design a comprehensive assessment? What are the resources needed to support assessment work?

2. How is concern for stakeholders reflected in organizational culture? What do the core values of the organization express about employees and other stakeholders?

3. Can you identify areas of trust in concern for stakeholders? Can you identify areas of distrust in concern for stakeholders? What can you learn from these examples?

4. Do your stakeholders trust the organization's concern for them? What can you learn from their answers?

5. Do you have any concerns for productivity and retention? Do your productivity results relate to concern for stakeholders? What does this mean for needed action?

Strategy Two: Assess Policies and Practices for Demonstration of Concern

Conduct a comprehensive audit of organizational practices, policies, and processes for demonstration of concern for stakeholders.

Earlier we discussed hiring, performance appraisal, salary administration, promotional practices, and grievance processes as examples of practices, policies, and processes related to trust in concern. Additionally, we described customer trust evaluations based on organizational interactions, ranging from service support to return policies. The areas we have listed are the types of practices, policies, and processes in need of review with an eye to assessing the "concern for stakeholder" messages embedded in each. The list will differ by organization. A comprehensive audit goes beyond the most obvious policies and practices to include conflict resolution, financial controls, reward and recognition programs, medical benefits, leave policies, and a host of other potentials. The audit is not designed to change organizational practices, policies, and processes, but first to understand their impact on trust. Sometimes change will be needed. At other times, clear communication about the policy, practice, or process will improve the trust profile.

Strategy Three: Communicate Concern for Stakeholders

Excel at communicating concern for stakeholders.

Gus Lee, in his provocative book *Courage*, identifies three things that courageous leaders learn to do well: respect and value others; provide support and encouragement; and challenge wrongs.[11] We believe these three areas for action are at the core of building trust in concern, whether for employees or for external stakeholders. Respect and value are determined through a host of communication interactions. How do leaders describe employees? How do supervisors deal with conflict and mistakes? Are employees "put in the middle" because of conflicting expectations? Are employees treated as if they are competent or incompetent? Do employees have contact with leaders? If not, what does that indicate about fundamental respect and value? Messages of support and encouragement occur daily in all types of interactions. Goal setting, performance appraisal, training, and a host of other less-obvious actions contribute to the support and encouragement individuals experience. Is credit given where credit is due? In other words, are people recognized for their contributions or do only senior people benefit when goals are met? Finally, is the organization vigilant about challenging and correcting wrongs. Internally or externally, addressing problems and correcting them rapidly expresses fundamental concern for stakeholders. Customers value problem resolution. Employees value problem resolution. Problem resolution contributes to excellent results. Excelling at communicating concern is in alignment with organizational goal achievement. Communicating respect, support, encouragement and challenging wrongs increase trust and measurable productivity.

Strategy Four: Align Communication, Policies, and Practices to Support Concern for Stakeholders

Excel at alignment.

Organizations excelling at alignment among intentions, behaviors, policies, and practices understand their trust profile and actively eliminate inconsistencies among intent, behaviors, and practices. Leaders at all levels are held accountable for developing consistency in messages, actions, and practices that reflects a genuine caring for stakeholders. Policies and practices are developed with a commitment to achieving goals through employees, vendors, customers, clients, investors, or donors, not in spite of these important stakeholders. Assessments of alignment should be conducted periodically, with revisions made as needed. We know from experience that this is easier said than done. We also know the vast majority of leaders want to express concern for stakeholders. However, it is uncommon to find organizations that regularly assess their communication, policies, and practices. We emphasize this strategy because it is an uncommon practice that pays rich dividends.

The following list provides questions leaders can ask for building trust in concern for stakeholders.

Questions for Building Trust in Organizational Concern for Stakeholders
Assessment of Concern for Stakeholders and Trust in Concern for Stakeholders

1. How can our organization assess our current concern for our stakeholders?

2. How can our organization assess the trust our stakeholders have in our concern for them?

3. Who should be responsible for these assessments?

Assessment of Policies and Practices for Demonstration of Concern

1. Which practices, policies, and processes should be identified for assessment?

2. Which practices, policies, and processes are most important to our employees?

3. Which practices, policies, and processes are most important to our customers/clients?

4. Which practices, policies, and processes are most important to other key stakeholders?

5. What criteria will we use to assess how our practices, policies, and processes demonstrate concern?

Communication of Concern for Stakeholders

1. Do our core values respect and value our stakeholders? Provide support and encouragement? Challenge wrongs?

2. What are our strengths in communicating concern for our stakeholders?

3. What are our weaknesses in communicating concern for our stakeholders?

4. What should change to improve our performance?

5. Who should be responsible for improvements?

Alignment to Support Concern for Stakeholders

1. Where are we consistent in our alignment to demonstrate concern among intent, behaviors, policies, practices, and processes?

2. Where are we inconsistent in our alignment to demonstrate concern?

3. How can we utilize our strengths to meet our challenges?

4. What should change?

5. What should stay the same?

6. Who is responsible for specific needed changes?

Trust in Action: Living by the Little Yellow Book at CH2M HILL

CH2M HILL is a global provider of engineering, procurement, construction, and operations services. In 1946, Fred Merryfield (an Oregon State University civil engineering professor) and Holly Cornell, James Howland, and T. Burke Hayes (former students of Merryfield's) established CH2M using their initials to form the company name. In 1971, the firm merged with Clair A. Hill & Associates to become CH2M HILL. Today the company employs over 25,000 people and generates annual revenue of more than $5 billion. Notable projects include the design and oversight of construction of the venues for the 2012 London Olympic and Paralympic games, development of Masdar City, the first carbon-neutral "green" community in Abu Dhabi in the United Arab Emirates, and program management for the expansion of the Panama Canal.

Since its inception, CH2M HILL has been 100 percent employee owned. The company has an internal stock market in which thirty-three million shares of stock are traded among employees. Stock values are fixed at three-month intervals by the company's board of directors. From 2000 through 2009, the value of the employee-owned stock increased from $4 per share to over $30 per share. At a time when other corporate portfolios have been rapidly losing value, CH2M HILL has had only three quarters in which employees experienced declines in stock value, resulting in a grand increase in value of 614 percent in the 2000s.[12]

CH2M HILL has been ranked several times on *Fortune* magazine's list of the "100 Best Companies to Work For," and in January 2009 CH2M HILL became the first engineering and construction firm to win the Catalyst Award, which honors innovative organizational approaches that address the recruitment, development, and advancement of women, including women of color. As Lee McIntire, CH2M HILL's chief executive officer explains, "This accomplishment was possible because of our people and their dedication to our company, our customers, and each other. Our ranking is the result of our employee-ownership culture, our commitment to develop our people, and our ability to provide them with an innovative, challenging, and high-integrity environment in which they can grow, learn, and excel in their careers."[13]

CH2M HILL employees often cite the opportunity to work on interesting projects that challenge their professional skills and improve the quality of the life in their communities as key reasons for joining and staying with the company. Employees also are afforded the opportunity to participate in comprehensive and ongoing training and professional development programs (on average, each full-time employee at CH2M HILL participates in sixteen hours of training annually) and work/life balance programs (10 percent of employees take advantage of CH2M HILL's flexible work schedules by working compressed weeks, and 5 percent of employees telework).[14]

The backbone of the company is a philosophy that was outlined by company founder Jim Howland, known as the Little Yellow Book. The Little Yellow Book is given to every new employee and subcontractor, and posters with pages from the fourteen-page book are found throughout CH2M HILL offices. Although the messages in the Little Yellow Book are simple, the impact is profound in shaping a culture of trust based on concern for employees. Some of Howland's thoughts on how CH2M HILL staff should behave include:

> "A good test to determine if a contemplated action is ethical is to ask, 'Would I want to see it in the headlines tomorrow morning?'
>
> "Avoid position perks such as parking spaces reserved for individuals, thick rugs, swivel thrones, and oversized offices.
>
> "Let's everybody be generous. It is especially important that those at or near the top of the heap be willing to spread the returns in dollars and recognition around."[15]

Chapter Lessons in Trust

1. Genuine caring for employees, customers, and other stakeholders characterizes the high-trust organization.

2. Trust in concern for stakeholders is directly related to employee satisfaction and overall organizational effectiveness.

3. Employees are more productive when organizations care about their well-being.

4. Customers are more loyal to organizations that care about their needs.

5. Caring and concern inspire trust and are of mutual benefit to the organization and stakeholders.

6. Distrust in concern reduces employee productivity and retention.

7. Distrust results from not respecting, valuing, encouraging, or supporting employees and other stakeholders.

8. Distrust results from not addressing wrongs.

9. Building trust begins with an assessment of communication practices, policies, and processes important to demonstrate concern for stakeholders.

10. Trust in concern requires alignment of intentions, behaviors, policies, and practices to support concern for stakeholders.

6

TRUST AND ORGANIZATIONAL RELIABILITY

"You miss 100 percent of the shots you don't take."
—*Wayne Gretzky, former NHL player*
and coach of the Phoenix Coyotes

Many CEOs and most public relations executives are not terribly excited when their organizations are described as reliable. Reliable is good, but not a description considered important for establishing distinctiveness. While we understand this perspective, reliability is one of the critical dimensions in our trust model. Without reliability, organizations lower their trust profiles and endanger the very excellence and distinctiveness they seek. Reliable organizations align their words and actions, follow through on commitments, exhibit consistent performance, engage in continuous improvement, ensure procedural fairness, and take responsibility for actions and outcomes. Some confuse sameness or the status quo with reliability. The reliable organization does not cling to the status quo and does foster positive change. The reliable organization provides consistent or "reliable" explanations in support of productive change and goal achievement.

The Reliable Organization

Drummond Manufacturing is a good example of a successful organization with a high reliability profile. With an overwhelming U.S. market share, privately owned Drummond has for the past eighty-five years dominated segments of the plumbing business with its washers and valves.[1] Known for its consistent product quality, service to customers, and dedicated employees, Drummond has not been challenged by global competitors, unlike most of its industry.

We learned from Jim Drummond, president and son of the founder, about the steadiness, fairness, and transparency needed for others to have high trust in the reliability of Drummond Manufacturing. Drummond told us, "Reputation is key. Consistent quality is the foundation of our success. We knock ourselves out— you can count on us, we say what we mean, and mean what we say. It is hard sometimes because rewards come slowly. Too many people become inconsistent because they manage to the fast and now. We recruit people who do work really well. Some people when they hit a demanding organization stay and grow; some don't. We have built our culture around excellence and striving for perfection. Our next generation of leaders has all been with us over fifteen years. They know our culture and core values. We are committed to them and their success." Drummond underscored for us the importance of leadership accountability and the honoring of commitments both within and external to the organization. He made an important distinction between reliability and the need for timely change. "We have had to change direction with new products and with the demands of new technologies. We have been through several severe economic downturns. We always tell the truth. We tell our people when we don't know. We don't predict the future." We learned from Drummond what is supported by a vast amount of research, including our own: reliability is fundamental to help people commit to excellence, even during times of challenge and change.

Trust in Reliability

> "Whoever can be trusted with very little can also be
> trusted with very much, and whoever is dishonest
> with very little will also be dishonest with much."
> —Luke, *physician and apostle, died c. 84 A.D.*

Trust in reliability comes from individual and macro-organizational experiences. Employees determine whether their supervisors follow through with what they say they are going to do. They watch to see whether or not their supervisors behave consistently from day to day. They evaluate the degree to which commitments are kept. Trust in top leaders is based in part on evaluations of whether or not individuals at the top keep their commitments to employees and other important stakeholders.

Organizations with consistent positive performance results are trusted for their reliability. Not surprisingly, organizations with varying performance results have lower trust profiles. Professional sports teams and symphony orchestras are similar in the examples they provide. Winning teams and famous orchestras are trusted for their consistently reliable high levels of performance. Most people do not pay top dollar to witness inconsistent and marginal talent.

Timely response to stakeholder needs is another dimension of reliability contributing to trust. We measure the effectiveness of first responders (police, fire, medical) by the amount of time it takes to respond to emergency calls. Customers want timeliness and reliability in service support and in the quality of the products or services they purchase. Organizations are evaluated for their reliability in addressing problems consistently across various stakeholders. High trust in organizational reliability promotes employee satisfaction and perceptions of organizational effectiveness. High trust in reliability assists organizations in working through crises and problems. When crises and problems arise, stakeholders trust, based on prior experiences, the reliable organization to have the ability to meet present challenges.

Distrust in Reliability

"Trust is a small word with major meaning. More importantly, as grandma used to say: Trust takes a lifetime to earn and can be lost in the blink of an eye."

—William Locander and David Luechauer,
professors of leadership at the Davis College
of Business at Jacksonville University

Distrust in reliability lowers employee satisfaction and customer or client loyalty, resulting in negative or at best skeptical perceptions of organizational effectiveness. Distrust results when stakeholders believe abuses of power, hidden agendas, and self-interest trump reliable, ethical, and transparent behaviors. Distrust in reliability increases when commitments are not kept without adequate explanations for change. Distrust grows when supervisors or top leaders do not do what they say they are going to do or honor commitments. Distrust is prevalent in situations when employees or other stakeholders believe unfair or unequal treatment is in evidence. Compensation practices, rewards, and advancement opportunities are some of the more important organizational processes whereby employees evaluate whether or not reliable, fair practices have been followed. Customers, clients, or vendors distrust organizations in which inconsistent responses to service needs or inconsistent responses to questions about requirements are prevalent. Investors or donors distrust organizations with inconsistent or unreliable performance results. Simply put, distrust in reliability contributes to lower performance and lower satisfaction with the organization.

One of our clients, the brilliant CEO of a leading educational products developer, helps illustrate what happens when distrust in reliability grows. Our client, Linda Smither, was aggressive, abrupt, and future-thinking. She had been named CEO of Western Educational Corporation with a mandate from the board of directors to grow its customer base and develop new programs expanding the traditional strengths of the company. The board hired us to assist her with strategic planning. Our first meeting with Linda began with us discussing various options for strategic planning.[2] Linda quickly stated she trusted few and wanted only a small group of close advisors. We asked why. Linda told us she thought most people resisted major change and would work to actively obstruct progress. She believed this attitude would be particularly prevalent at Western because of the company's long commitment to a limited but excellent product line and the long tenure of most of the senior leadership team. We voiced our concern about a process that was not inclusive, believing it was likely to meet resistance and distrust. Over the next several weeks, Linda's public comments about the strategic planning process seemed to indicate she agreed with our recommendation about inclusive planning. She formed task teams headed by senior leadership, with team members drawn from product development, marketing, communications, human resources, and finance and administration. Each team had a clear charge and timeline. Linda also began work on the plan with a selected few senior individuals and a friend from her previous employer. When the task teams presented their work, Linda thanked team members and complimented the quality of the reports. Linda did not provide a timeline for the next steps for preparing the final plan. We suggested it was important she communicate next steps and timing to the entire organization. She agreed. Several weeks passed with no communication about the plan to senior leadership or the entire organization. Key leadership team members expressed frustration, and two reported she had "dressed them down" severely when they asked about the plan's status. At the next regularly scheduled board meeting, Linda presented the strategic plan without having previously shared it with the senior leadership team or others in the organization. It was not clear who, if anyone, in the organization had seen the final draft. The plan called for sweeping reorganization of product development and marketing. New programs were targeted for development, and new marketing strategies were planned. The board endorsed the plan, to the amazement of the senior leaders, who were surprised by Linda's presentation and in disagreement with major components of her strategy. We told Linda we could not continue to advise her because of the contradiction between what she was doing and what she had said she was going to do. She agreed she had not been consistent (reliable) and asked us to facilitate a meeting with her senior leadership team. She wanted to explain to them why she had kept the plan a secret and how her next steps would be more inclusive. The meeting illustrated the damage from distrust. Linda began the meeting by explaining she had been charged by the board to bring about major change and she knew not everyone would welcome the extent of change she intended to make. She stated she valued the work they had produced in the task teams and now wanted to include them in implementing the changes. The director of marketing challenged the approach to marketing presented in the plan. Linda dismissed his concerns abruptly. We knew from the interaction in the meeting that Linda had no commitment from her leadership team to the plan, although all agreed they would begin implementation. Linda indicated she would release the plan to the entire organization and asked for their support. No one responded.

Linda's internal communication to all employees stressed the broad involvement from the task teams in the creation of the strategic plan. She thanked leadership and team members for their hard work and asked for cooperation in the implementation stages. She asked for input from all employees to assist in bringing about changes in their specific areas. Over the next two weeks, Linda received several specific recommendations from employee groups. She did not respond. We talked with her about the lack of alignment between her words and actions. Again, she agreed. (We believed she was simply agreeing rather than addressing the issues we raised. We resigned from the account.)

Within six months, four members of the senior leadership team had written a letter to the president of the board indicating they no longer had confidence in Linda. They detailed the planning process and the contradiction between Linda's statements and the manner in which the plan had been developed. They cited specific flaws in the plan. Turnover rates among product developers increased, with one developer stating in a public email to company employees his distrust of what was happening between the CEO and her leadership team. Linda was asked by the board to resign.

So why is the distrust of Linda related to our reliability trust dimension and not a host of other potential factors? We agree reliability does not operate in isolation from openness and honesty, integrity, or a variety of leadership and communication styles. We believe, however, that Linda's case illustrates reliability because of the pattern of inconsistency between her words and actions. Many of her senior leaders agreed elements of the plan were brilliant, but they no longer could count on her to do what she said she was going to do. They viewed her has having hidden agendas and putting self-interest ahead of her commitments to them and all employees. One senior manager summed it up when he said, "Linda changes from day to day. You never know which Linda is going to show up in the morning. It is not productive to work that way."

This example illustrates the cost of distrust not only for Linda but for Western Educational Corporation. Linda's termination derailed what had been a career marked by increasing levels of responsibility. She did not work again for two years and was finally offered a job at a substantially lower salary and position level. Western did not implement the strategic plan and experienced declining revenues over the next two years. Analysts credited the decline to the lack of new products in an increasingly competitive market. A new CEO for Western pursued a more inclusive planning process and many of the original plan ideas were incorporated into an effort, which was launched approximately three years following the initial board mandate for change. The new products were excellent but late to the market, impacting profits for at least five years. Our Western example illustrates the lingering impact of distrust and the importance of incorporating trust building in all strategic change efforts.

Reliability works together with competence, openness and honesty, and concern for stakeholders in support of building trust necessary for excellence. Next we turn to specific strategies for building trust in reliability.

Building Trust in Reliability

"Building trust is like free mountain climbing—one slip and you're dead."
—David Arnott, *researcher at Warwick Business School at the University of Warwick, Coventry, UK*

Building trust in reliability, as with the other dimensions of our model, requires an understanding of the behaviors, processes, and performance required for an organization to be evaluated as reliable. Trust in reliability is an alignment between words and actions; it is consistency across situations; it is consistency over time; it is keeping commitments; it is fairness of processes; and it is sustained high-quality performance.

Strategies for Building Trust in Reliability

"Steadiness during turbulence is what we need. I believe we will have a better future because I work with reliable people."
—*Anonymous educational leader*

The trust-building strategies we present here are designed to align organizational words and actions and develop consistency important for high performance.

Strategy One: Assess Reliability and Trust in Reliability

Conduct a complete and thoughtful assessment of the current state of reliability throughout the organization and the extent to which stakeholders trust the reliability of the organization.

Key questions should be developed with a commitment to listen and act on the answers. Key questions include:

1. What department and which individuals have the expertise to design a comprehensive assessment? What are the resources needed to support assessment work?

2. Does the organizational culture support reliability?

3. Can you identify specific examples of trust in reliability? Are there examples of distrust in reliability? What can you learn from these examples?

4. Does the organization behave consistently across similar situations? If so, what is the result? If not, what is the result?

5. Is the organization trusted to behave consistently over time? If so, what is the result? If not, what is the result?

6. Do stakeholders trust in the performance results of the organization? If not, how does distrust impact the present and future?

It is important to assess perceptions of what constitutes reliable behavior when communicating across cultures. One particularly challenging example involves business communication among Americans and the Chinese. As John Graham and Mark Lam explain in their discussion of the expectations of the Chinese in business negotiations, "All too often, Americans see Chinese negotiators as inefficient, indirect, and even dishonest, while the Chinese see American negotiators as aggressive, impersonal, and excitable."[3] While providing logically organized and detailed information, communicating directly, and forging a good deal may be viewed as reliable behaviors in the United States, Chinese executives are more likely to view a process-oriented interaction (often involving intermediaries) designed to develop a long-term relationship as most desirable. These personal relationships or connections, called *guanxi* in China, are at the heart of building trust in reliability. Good guanxi depends on a system of reciprocity, or what the Chinese call *hui bao*. This is not immediate reciprocity in the sense that Chinese businesspeople will offer concessions directly after such allowances have been made by others, but rather a long-term sense of personal obligation. As Graham and Lam explain, "Ignoring reciprocity in China is not just bad manners; it's immoral. [Such behavior] poisons the well for all future business."[4]

Further, those in the United States often find it difficult to grasp the level of hierarchical and formal structure in Chinese business. Consider the example of a U.S. company that sent a younger, low-level sales representative to a high-level Chinese business negotiation. The Chinese executive commented to his American counterpart, "You're about the same age as my son." This was not a statement of parental pride, but rather an indication the Chinese business executive felt insulted by the Americans' unwillingness to send a representative of equal rank and status to participate in the negotiation. This action called the American company's sincerity into question. The resulting perception that the American organization just wasn't reliable enough to do business with ended conversation before serious negotiations could begin.

Both the notion of guanxi and the importance of respecting the Chinese value on hierarchy and status came into play when General Motors and Ford were seeking entry into the Chinese automotive market in the mid-1990s. GM CEO John F. Smith made three trips to Beijing to meet with Chinese executives. GM also utilized a Shanghai-born, fluent Mandarin speaker (who had great guanxi) as their liaison in China. At the same time, Ford appointed Jim Paulsen, an American engineer, as its point person in China. Paulsen and his team lacked a sufficient understanding of Chinese culture and language. As a result, General Motors, selling vehicles under the Buick, Chevrolet, Opel, Saab, and Cadillac names, is the best-selling foreign automaker in China, while Ford continues to struggle to get a foothold in the Chinese market.[5] The reason for this is quite simple: Chinese executives perceived GM as a more reliable and trustworthy business partner.

Strategy Two: Develop a Culture of Reliability

Excel at aligning words and actions.

The high-reliability organization has a culture of alignment. All levels of management are responsible for keeping commitments or providing explanations for changes. Care is taken to not over-commit to either employees or other stakeholders. Even with explanations for change, a pattern of breaking commitments lowers the trust profile of the organization. A culture of reliability focuses on consistently solving problems and bringing closure to issues of importance to stakeholders. Continuous feedback and improvement are important characteristics of the reliable culture. Finally, reliable high-quality performance results support trust in reliability.

Strategy Three: Promote Accountability

Excel at taking responsibility for results.

Communicating clear performance expectations throughout the organization is fundamental for establishing broad-based accountability. Promoting accountability requires examining performance expectations for top leadership and determining how those expectations are met and translated into expectations throughout the organization. All employees should be able to identify how their performance fits into the overall results expectations of the organization. Promoting accountability requires support for individuals taking responsibility, regardless of their job positions. Blame is avoided, encouraging individuals to admit mistakes, offer solutions to problems, and work for positive change beyond their specific job duties. Finally, an organization which promotes accountability has leaders who take personal responsibility for results while providing inclusive credit for high performance.

One multinational company that has been very adept at promoting accountability is McDonald's. While the signature McDonald's sandwich, the Big Mac, is served in much the same way around the globe, McDonald's also serves regional items such as kosher hamburgers in Israel, vegetable McNuggets in India, sandwiches on rye bread in Finland, teriyaki beef in Japan, and the Kiwi Burger—a local favorite featuring a fried egg and beetroot—in New Zealand. Unlike many other large global corporations, McDonald's restaurants mostly are locally owned—affording restaurant franchisees an intimate understanding of regional culture and promoting accountability to employees and customers. In Muslim countries, McDonald's offers prayer rooms, while in Greece it significantly alters its menu during Lent. In Asia, students often sit in McDonald's for hours—turning the restaurants into youth clubs—a practice that would not be tolerated in the United States but is encouraged by local owners in places like Hong Kong, Seoul, and Beijing.

This adaptation to local customs by a globally branded company has been dubbed "glocalization." Of course, much of the McDonald's experience is standardized around the globe—from the golden arches to the core menu items—making dining at McDonald's much the same from Atlanta to Nairobi to Warsaw. Entrepreneurs from all over the world are taught McDonald's product and service-quality principles at one of four Hamburger Universities. This encourages that consistent, reliable quality standards are maintained among McDonald's outlets around the globe. At the same time, local owners are given wide latitude to adapt the McDonald's concept to their native cultures. The results have been positive. McDonald's sales in the United States have been on the increase after declines in previous years. The company is doing well in other parts of the world as well. Sales increased in the first half of 2009 by nearly 7 percent, with much of that growth coming in Europe and Asia. France, somewhat surprisingly, is outpacing performance in most markets around the world. McDonald's has been successful in winning over French consumers, with restaurants featuring barstools made from bicycle seats and wood-and-stone interiors reminiscent of a chalet. Further, French customers spend an average of $9 per visit, compared to only $4 in the United States, even though a Big Mac costs roughly the same in Paris and New York. In Germany, supermodel Heidi Klum has served as a spokesperson for the company. The emphasis of her campaign was on the restaurant chain's commitment to fitness and health. McDonald's financial future will depend on its continuing ability to connect with global customers. The company serves fifty million people every day in about 31,000 restaurants in 119 countries. To continue to increase sales volume, McDonald's will need to continue to suit the tastes of customers around the world by acknowledging local cuisine and culture and encouraging accountability in meeting performance standards from its franchisees around the world. [6]

Strategy Four: Foster Transparency

Excel at communicating organizational expectations, processes, and results.

Reliability is established through consistent communication that makes transparent the day-to-day workings of the organization. How are hiring processes understood? Are they perceived to be fair and effective? Do all employees have clear and realistic performance expectations? Do stakeholders know what is expected of top leaders? How are decisions communicated? Are decisions consistent across situations? Is information about change provided in a timely manner and with regard to the interests of multiple stakeholders? Does the organization regularly address problems and bring closure to issues of concern? How are overall results and achievements presented?

Transparency contributes to high trust in reliability because stakeholders consistently can access what they need to know about the organization and what the organization wants them to know about changing circumstances. Transparency lowers distrust through regular, clear information exchanges. Transparency supports continuing feedback to the organization from a variety of internal and external stakeholders.

Aligning words and deeds is particularly important in times of crisis. We have worked over the years with several organizations that have had to deal with varying calamities, ranging from severe financial pressures to product failures and public ethical breaches. Although our trust dimension of openness and honesty, among other dimensions, is critical in these situations, it is often reliability that is overlooked in dealing with such crises. It is absolutely essential that organizational leaders engage in consistent, reliable behavior in difficult circumstances. Two clients we worked with provide an excellent contrast.

Several years ago we worked with a client with very ambitious growth goals. This particular division was vital to the overall profitability of its parent company, and the targets for expanding the business were often in double digits every year. The challenge of growing a business at this rate was very demanding on the leaders of the organization and on the frontline staff responsible for day-to-day operation of the business. Most were working long hours, including many evenings and weekends. When year-end figures were reported at a town hall meeting we attended, the data presented indicated there had been significant growth over the past year, but the growth was not at the level expected by the parent company. Increases that might have been a cause for celebration in other organizations were being reported as a failure in this meeting. Further, it was explained that, by missing the growth targets set by the parent company, this division would have to tighten its belt and get serious about cutting costs. There would be no bonuses in the coming year, and pay raises and other benefits would be scaled back. As you can imagine, the mood at the end of the town hall meeting was somber. Despite this, morale within the division was quite good, and employees indicated they were willing to work even harder to meet the ambitious goals that had been outlined. The positive mood changed rapidly, however, when leaders in the organization engaged in behaviors producing distrust in reliability. While employees struggled to make ends meet without their anticipated bonuses and pay increases, senior leaders held a strategic planning retreat at a posh resort, dined at expensive restaurants at company expense, and made seemingly frivolous travel to visit other divisions located in desirable parts of the world. This lack of reliability produced toxic reactions among the rank-and-file. Employees who had been willing to work harder to help the division meet its ambitious growth targets were suddenly balking at working on evenings and weekends; turnover increased dramatically; and productivity suffered. The inconsistent actions of the division leaders resulted in even further gaps between the parent company's growth goals for the division and actual results. We worked with the senior leaders in this organization to overcome the distrust in reliability that developed, but the damage had been done. We were eventually able to help to improve the situation, but it took a sustained, concerted effort to reenergize the demoralized workforce.

We saw the opposite with another client. In this organization there had been two significant financial downturns in an eight-year period. In both cases, the external economic climate significantly impacted the budget of the organization. In the first downturn, the leader of the organization went on the offensive, holding open forums to explain the situation to employees. She answered all questions openly and honestly and provided all the information available, indicating what she knew and didn't know and could and could not predict. Just as importantly, this leader behaved reliably in all that she did. She told her employees that she would cut budgets (starting with her own) to avoid layoffs. And while other competitors did engage in layoffs, she held true to her promise to maintain employment for all in the organization. Although some of the cuts were painful and not everyone was happy with all of the decisions she made, none of the employees felt the leader had exhibited distrust in reliability. Even if the message was hard to accept, her actions were clear and consistent. This first crisis set the stage for the second economic downturn that occurred eight years later. Again, we saw the leader conduct open forums to explain her strategy to avoid layoffs. She referred back to her past actions from nearly a decade earlier to build trust in reliability. And what we observed was incredible. Where there had been considerable discontent in the first round of budget cuts eight years ago, there were absolutely no complaints this time around. We observed the leader meet with over five hundred employees and, amazingly, not one employee questioned the leader's strategy, integrity, or motives. The trust in reliability was almost universal.

What do these two examples tell us? They suggest that, even if you are completely open and honest with employees, you cannot fully gain trust unless you also are reliable.

The following list presents questions for building trust in reliability.

Questions for Building Trust in Reliability
Assessment of Reliability and Trust in Reliability

1. How can our organization assess our current reliability?

2. How can our organization assess the trust our stakeholders have in our reliability?

3. Who should be responsible for these assessments?

Develop a Culture of Reliability

1. Does our culture support organizational reliability?

2. Do we hold leadership responsible for keeping commitments?

3. Do we solve problems with consistency and fairness?

4. How do we ensure we receive feedback from stakeholders and engage in continuous improvement?

5. What do our results say about our reliability?

Promote Accountability

1. Do we communicate clear performance expectations?

2. Do all employees understand how their performance expectations contribute to overall organizational results?

3. Do we promote problem resolution and avoid blame?

4. Do we take personal responsibility for organizational performance?

Foster Transparency

1. Do our communication processes make transparent the day-to-day operations of the organization?

2. Do stakeholders understand the expectations of top leaders?

3. Is information consistent across stakeholders?

4. Do we communicate how problems and issues are handled and resolved?

5. Do stakeholders have the information they need, and can they provide regular input to the organization?

Trust in Action: Achieving Customer Service Excellence at USAA

USAA provides insurance, investment, and banking services to over five-and-one-half million members around the world. The company employs nearly 22,000 people and has owned and managed assets exceeding $96 billion. Founded in 1922,

USAA originally provided automobile insurance to Army offi-
cers who had difficulty maintain coverage because of their frequent moves. Today the company serves U.S. military staff in
both enlisted and officer ranks in all service branches, offering
membership to active duty personnel, retirees, and their families. USAA has been recognized for its outstanding financial
performance and customer service. The company consistently
receives high ratings from all three major financial analysis
agencies—A.M. Best, Moody's, and Standard & Poor's, and was
ranked by BusinessWeek as number one on its list of Customer
Service Champs in 2007 and 2008 and number two in 2009.[7]

So how does USAA maintain this level of performance?
According to Vic Andrews, the recently retired vice president
and general manager of USAA's Mountain States Regional
Office in Colorado Springs, "USAA has always been very cus-
tomer-centric, although there was a period of time in the late
1990s to early 2000s where customer service was not as good as
it had been in the past. We decided in 2002 that we had to get
back to our emphasis on customer service. We focused on our
managers, each of whom has twelve to fourteen direct reports.
We told our managers we wanted them to spend the majority of
their time mentoring their twelve to fourteen direct reports by
listening to telephone calls—reinforcing what customer service
representatives were doing well and coaching them when they
could improve. In particular, we asked our managers to rein-
force how much authority our customer service representatives
had in ensuring the satisfaction of our members. We wanted to
be certain we were delivering world-class customer service. We
were very consistent, and nobody was confused that our primary
emphasis as an organization was on customer service. It took a
few years, but the message became clear."

The organization's emphasis in customer service is unswerv-
ing. USAA's service representatives, who make up 60 percent of
the company's employees, aren't scripted and their calls aren't
timed.[8] The results are evident in evaluations from Forrester

Research, J.D. Power, and *BusinessWeek*, all of whom rate USAA as outstanding. As Andrews explains, "What is so neat about the *BusinessWeek* ranking is that customers decide. It's not some committee, but our members who tell us we are doing a good job. We celebrated our Customer Service Champs ranking and told our employees 'This is about you.' The trophy went to every one of the six locations in the company. There was no management credit taken for the award. It was each and every person who talks with our members on the telephone who made that happen. We use a model at USAA called the three-legged stool. The three legs on the stool are members, employees, and financials. All three legs have to have equal attention or the stool won't stand. No one leg of the stool is more important or gets more emphasis."

The focus on customer service at USAA is consistent from the top of the organization all the way down to first-line employees. As Andrews describes it, "We believe our members. A real simple example of this is when a member calls us and says, 'My child is sixteen years old and is a high-school honors students' That results in a discount. We say, 'Fine, thank you very much' and we give the discount. We don't require the member to send in the student's report card; we don't ask for a letter from his or her principal; we just believe because, as a USAA member, until you prove otherwise, we believe what you say. Another example was the recent California fires. When a house burns down, the typical insurance company will ask the customer to make a list of everything that was in the house. When our CEO went to California and saw these houses burned to the ground, he said, 'Why would we be asking people what was in their house? They have this amount of coverage and everything is gone. Let's just write them a check.' So if you had $500,000 worth of coverage for your house and $300,000 worth of coverage for contents, we would write a check for $800,000 less the deductible and hand it to the member on the spot. It's about trust. We trust the member and they trust us."

As Andrews learned throughout his thirty-year career as an Air Force officer and in his time at USAA, "By being reliable as a leader, you build up a bank account of good will. You instill confidence in your followers that you can do the job." The only way to succeed in creating this environment is to listen to the concerns of followers and look for ways to continuously improve performance. For Andrews that meant regular interaction with his staff. "I would take a random sample of fifteen to twenty employees and invite them to breakfast each month. I would sit down with them and ask 'What would you like to talk about?' It's amazing. Sometimes it took some time before the first question was asked, but once the employees got started, it always produced a very beneficial dialogue. Sometimes I was asked a question and I had no idea, but I guarantee I would find out the answer and get back to that employee. Other times employees would ask a question and I knew they were not going to like the answer to the question, but I had to give them the honest answer and the explanation why we did it that way. It was great when an employee brought a problem to my attention and I could fix it. It would have been great if we could have fixed it before, but at least we could fix it once I became aware. People see that and they know they have a voice. It's important that people see you as a leader as a real person, a person they can talk to. When I was at USAA, I had about one thousand employees in my regional office. My goal was to interact with every person in the organization every week. That might just mean making eye contact because some of the employees spent the majority of their time on the telephone, but if I had an opportunity to stop by and start a conversation about the pictures in their cubicle or say 'How are you doing?' I would do that while I was making my rounds. As a [leader of a] customer service organization, I felt it was my responsibility to model customer service in my interactions with employees. I also spoke to every new employee who came into the organization during orientation and I would tell him or her, 'You are my customer. Your customers are outside the organization on the other end of the telephone or the email you receive, but you are my customer. My job is to provide you with the environment so that you can serve your customers.'"[9]

Chapter Lessons in Trust

1. Trust in reliability is fundamental for high performance.

2. Reliability is based on alignment of words and actions, honoring of commitments, consistent performance, continuous improvement, procedural fairness, and responsibility for actions and outcomes.

3. Trust in reliability is necessary for overall stakeholder satisfaction and perceptions of organizational effectiveness.

4. Distrust in reliability results from broken commitments, power abuses, hidden agendas, and perceptions of self-interest trumping reliable, ethical, and transparent behaviors.

5. Building trust in reliability is based on a thoughtful understanding of the alignment of organizational words and actions and perceptions of stakeholder trust in reliability.

6. Top leaders are responsible for modeling alignment of words and actions, honoring commitments, and taking responsibility for results.

7. Developing a culture of reliability positively increases an organization's trust profile.

8. Promoting accountability throughout the organization increases trust in reliability and contributes to high performance.

9. Fostering transparency includes communicating about organizational expectations, processes, and results and providing multiple avenues for feedback to the organization.

10. A culture of reliability, accountability, and transparency contributes to high-performance results.

7

TRUST AND ORGANIZATIONAL IDENTIFICATION

"Positioning the brand and regaining trust are all
smart things for us to do and those are the litmus
tests for any decisions we make."
—*John McKinley, chief technology officer for
AOL LLC (formerly America Online, Inc.)*

Organizations with high trust profiles are strong identification organizations. Employees, customers, vendors, and other stakeholders value what the organization values and feel a sense of connection to the organization. Identification, simply put, is the affiliation, association, or attachment individuals experience with a variety of organizations when they interpret their relationships with organizations as interdependent with their needs, values, and conceptions of what is right. We understand identification when we remember our alma maters with affection, we voluntarily contribute time and money to philanthropic or religious institutions, and we connect to diverse political and social groups. We continually assess our identification with the organizations in which we work. We quickly realize identification and trust are inextricably linked. Most of us do not continue to affiliate with organizations in which there is not a strong sense of shared values, purpose, and mutually beneficial experiences.

The Strong Identification Organization

One organization that enjoys high levels of identification from both its employees and its customers is the retail chain,

Nordstrom. Nordstrom began as a small shoe store in Seattle in 1901 and has grown into a retail giant with more than one hundred large department stores and fifty outlet clearance centers (Nordstrom Rack) in the United States, thirty boutiques in Europe (Faconnable), and one of the top-rated online customer apparel companies (Nordstrom.com). Together they generate some $8 billion per year in sales. Although other retailers may be larger, few engender so much enthusiasm and loyalty from both customers and employees.

From the beginning, Nordstrom incorporated the idea that outstanding customer service offers a competitive advantage. Stories abound concerning the almost mythic levels of assistance provided by Nordstrom staff. This (well-deserved) reputation has turned the opening of new Nordstrom stores into civic events. When the first Nordstrom was built in Denver in the 1990s, hundreds of shoppers camped overnight in the parking lot in anticipation of the store's grand opening. Nordstrom capitalizes on this customer devotion, producing sales of about $400 per square foot—nearly double the sales for an average department store. Employee identification is also well above industry averages, with turnover rates that are infinitesimal compared to other similar retailers.

The key to Nordstrom's success is its leadership philosophy, based on trusting employees to do whatever it takes to satisfy customers. As in many companies, new hires at Nordstrom attend an employee orientation before they begin work on the sales floor. Unlike other companies, however, the training focuses almost exclusively on customer service. Each new hire is given a 5-inch by 7-inch card, entitled The Nordstrom Rule Book, which reads: "WELCOME TO NORDSTROM. We're glad to have you with our company. Our number one goal is to provide *outstanding customer service*. Set both your personal and professional goals high. We have great confidence in your ability to achieve them. Nordstrom Rules: Rule #1: *Use your good judgment in all situations*. There will be no additional rules. Please feel free to ask your department manager, store manager, or division general manager any questions at any time."[1]

This entrepreneurial spirit allows Nordstrom sales associates to perform at levels that often exceed customers' expectations. The liberal return and exchange policies at Nordstrom might invite abuse, but the company's unconditional money-back guarantee is built on the assumption that both employees and customers can be trusted. Indeed, one loyal Nordstrom customer we spoke to told us that he has not returned items he knew would be exchanged without question because he has "too much respect and loyalty to the company" to take advantage of the generous return policies.

Developing this level of employee and customer identification can be challenging. Nordstrom prefers to hire people without previous sales experience. As Jim Nordstrom, the late co-chairman of the company, once explained, those with little sales experience "haven't learned to say 'no' to customers, because they haven't worked for anybody else."[2] Nordstrom expects its sales staff to exhibit high levels of professionalism and initiative and pays its sales associates about 20 percent above industry standards. Most exceed their base pay rate by earning a higher commission-based pay of approximately 6.75 percent of their sales volume. In 2005, the company reported that seventy-six employees exceeded $1 million in sales. This allows Nordstrom staff the opportunity to earn exceptional salaries as their sales increase, benefiting both the employee and the bottom line at Nordstrom. Salespeople also receive full benefits, including retirement, medical and dental insurance, plus a variety of incentives supporting work and life balance.[3] As Nordstrom has learned, financial outcomes are best for the staff and for the company when both employees and customers strongly identify with the organization.

We find the Nordstrom example intriguing. We know identification when we experience it, but how does it really work? Identification occurs when we feel connected to our peers, immediate leaders, or the entire organization. Identification is based on having values similar to those of our peers and values similar to those of other leaders. Personal experience supports a large body of research which suggests individuals have value systems they continually contrast with the perceived value systems of the organizations where they work, contribute time and money, become customers, or provide services. In other words, the more individuals value what the organization values, the more likely individuals are satisfied with and have positive expectations about the organization. Individuals hold personal values, beliefs, and assumptions about ideal organizational life they continually contrast with their perceptions of organizational reality. The perceived *gap* between the ideal and perceived reality is pivotal for overall satisfaction with the organization and estimations of quality and overall effectiveness. Obviously, the smaller the gap, the more closely we identify with the organization.[4] Jim Collins and Jerry Porras, in their best seller, *Built to Last,* describe successful visionary companies as organizations with high identification.[5] According to Collins and Porras, visionary companies have a core ideology they spend considerable efforts in helping employees and all stakeholders to understand and embrace. Collins and Porras write "people tend to either fit well with the company and its ideology or tend to not fit at all ('buy in or get out')." They contend there is an elitism in high-performing companies that contributes to a sense of belonging to . . . "something special and superior."

Trust in Identification

"I was no chief and never had been, but because
I had been more deeply wronged than others, this
honor was conferred upon me, and I resolved to
prove worthy of the trust."
—Geronimo, *Apache Nation leader, 1829–1909*

In many respects, the identification dimension of our trust model emerges from experiences with the other model dimensions: competence, openness and honesty, concern for stakeholders, and reliability. Organizations do not enjoy strong identification when their competence, openness and honesty, concern for stakeholders, or reliability are in question. However, identification requires experiences beyond those surrounding the other four dimensions. Stakeholders experience strong identification with organizations when they share values and purpose and experience connection to organizational members, services, and products. Employees, in particular, experience strong identification when they believe, as Chun Hui and Cynthia Lee describe, "I count around here, and I am an important part of this place."[6] Not surprisingly, strong identification fosters quality and is related to employee and external stakeholder satisfaction with the organization and perceptions of effectiveness.[7]

Strong identification has additional benefits for the high-performing organization. Experience with our clients and extensive research support our view that strong organizational identification helps individuals cope during times of uncertainty. Trust in the values of an organization provides stakeholders the bonding it takes to work through difficulty. Loyalty resulting from strong identification literally buys time to deal with problems.

Anti-social behavior often increases with uncertainty. Rumors, negative conflict, and lower productivity all are associated with not knowing what is going to happen. Strong organizational identification does not eliminate uncertainty but it moderates the negatives, thereby contributing to the possibility of positive change.[8]

One organization that has very strong trust in identification from both its customers and employees is Zappos.com. Founded in 1999, Zappos increased its sales revenue from less than $1 million in its first year of operation to nearly $1 billion by 2008. With 1,400 employees, about half of whom work in the corporate headquarters in Las Vegas, and the remainder who work in nearly one million square feet of warehouse space near Louisville, Kentucky, the company describes itself as a "service company that happens to sell shoes, clothing, handbags, accessories, and eventually anything and everything."[9] In March 2009, we met with Zappos.com CEO Tony Hsieh and toured the Zappos headquarters while attending the Social Media for Communicators Conference in Las Vegas. Over 75 percent of sales at Zappos.com are from repeat customers. And why not? Zappos.com prides itself on providing the best customer service possible. While many online retailers make customers click through several pages to find the telephone number for customer service departments with limited hours of operation, Zappos offers 24/7 customer service support and puts its toll-free customer service number on the top of every page on its website. The company also offers free shipping, free returns, and a 365-day no-hassle return policy.

As Hsieh explains, "We have no call time metrics at Zappos. The telephone is one of the best branding devices available." Customer service representatives are trusted to spend as long as needed to satisfy their customers. "Our longest call was four hours," Hsieh adds. As long as customers have a WOW experience and employees are friendly, helpful, and go "above and beyond," Hsieh and his managers at Zappos encourage any creative effort that supports the organization's commitment to world-class service.

"Our number-one priority is company culture. If you get the culture right, everything else follows," according to Hsieh. The culture at Zappos is so well defined. There is a nearly 500-page "culture book" written by the employees and published each year. The book is displayed in the Zappos lobby and is given free of charge to the visitors who flock to the Las Vegas headquarters for tours. But it's not only loyal customers who visit the headquarters, corporate bench markers from such companies as Southwest Airlines and LEGO come to observe Zappos' commitment to customer service in action.

The cornerstone of the culture at Zappos is its "committable" core values:

1. Deliver WOW through service.
2. Embrace and drive change.
3. Create fun and a little weirdness.
4. Be adventurous, creative, and open-minded.
5. Pursue growth and learning.
6. Build open and honest relationships with communication.
7. Build a positive team and family spirit.
8. Do more with less.
9. Be passionate and determined.
10. Be humble.

To ensure the core values are shared among all of its employees, Zappos has an extensive four-week corporate culture training program. At the end of the first week, new hires are offered $2,000 to quit. Despite the fact that call-center workers in the area earn only about $11 an hour to start, in 2008 less than 1 percent accepted the offer to quit. "One thing we didn't plan for was that, by not taking the offer, our new hires became more committed to the company," explains Hsieh. This commitment to the company values and culture is carefully considered in the hiring process. "Zappos asks unusual questions in the interview process, such as on a scale from 1 to 10, how weird are you? We're not looking for a specific number, but we know if they rate themselves as a 1, they are too straight-laced; if they rate themselves as a 10, they may be too psychotic. We celebrate individuality; that's why we have no scripts for our customer service representatives," explains Hsieh.[10]

Another key tenet of the Zappos culture is transparency. Customers are welcome to tour the Las Vegas headquarters and they are told the experience will be unlike any other corporate tour they are likely to experience. Visitors are given gifts, photographed on a throne for the VIP Wall of Fame, and entertained by the proudly weird Zappos employees, including the c-suite leaders at Zappos, whose cubicles are in what is called monkey row—a rain-forest-themed workspace in the heart of the Las Vegas headquarters. All of this is unlike many other organizations, but it serves to build tremendous identification with both the Zappos brand and culture. In July 2009, Zappos announced it was being purchased by Amazon.com. Although the details are still to be worked out, Zappos will retain its staff (including Hsieh and his executive team) and unique culture. As Amazon CEO Jeff Bezos explained in a YouTube post announcing the acquisition, "Zappos has a totally unique culture. The culture and the Zappos brand are huge assets that I value, and I want to see those things continue."[11]

Although not as distinctive as Zappos, but equally telling, Martin Bartholomew, an intercultural communication trainer currently dividing his time between the United Kingdom and Latvia, described for us his experiences in two different organizations, one in which he failed to identify and another in which trust in his abilities resulted in strong identification. Bartholomew told us, "I was working in a large telecommunications company in Europe in a department that handled external communication with the marketplace. The company put a lot of effort into making us feel a part of the organization. Those efforts did not seem genuine and I could not connect with the organization, even though I respected the company as one of the best in the early 1990s. I felt that my contributions were not valued in the way I wanted them to be. I had been head hunted to work there and I wanted to help lead the organization, a skill for which I had been well trained, but they did not seem to trust me or respect that desire on my part. I did not identify in any way with the company, so I left. In another smaller organization, I was trusted as a mediator and a leader and put in a position that I was able to do what needed to be done in the marketplace. I was able to provide the stepping stones for other people to follow me, and they did. Because I was trusted, I identified with the organization and made my finest contributions to its goals."[12]

Distrust in Identification

"Suppliers, and especially manufacturers, have market power because they have information about a product or a service that the customer does not and cannot have, and does not need if he can trust the brand. This explains the profitability of brands."

—*Peter Drucker, author and business management theorist, 1909–2005*

Distrust in identification, or even a lack of identification, contributes not only to negative experiences but to decreased performance. When individuals cannot connect to an organization, they are more likely to pursue their own self-interests over the organization's interest. During times of uncertainty, distrust in identification fosters job insecurity, increased intentions to leave, absenteeism, and real productivity costs. Employees, customers, clients, investors, donors, and vendors who do not identify with an organization decrease their commitment, either in effort or money or both.

Distrust in identification is evidenced in resistance to change and a rise in antisocial behaviors. Lowered work effort, longer breaks, stealing, gossip, and verbal assaults are more prevalent when employees do not identify with their organizations. Individuals perceive more risk within an organization with which they do not identify. Downsizing, restructuring, and mergers often are met with negative reactions when stakeholders either distrust or have low organizational identification.[13]

One of our recent experiences illustrates the problem of distrust in identification. A fifty-year-old, private university changed presidents following the retirement of a long-serving popular leader who had increased enrollment, added programs, and grown the university's endowment five-fold. The faculty strongly disagreed with the governing board's choice of a new president, voicing fears the new individual would not uphold the values of the institution and did not have the academic credentials necessary for the job. The board chair released a statement to the media and the faculty and staff which stated, "The faculty are not running the university, they don't want the change we need, and we are totally supporting our choice." Pandemonium resulted. At the beginning of the fall semester, students and faculty protested outside the administration building. The media reported several key donors directed their displeasure to the board. After several weeks, the campus appeared to return to normal and the process of change began. The president announced elimination of several low-enrollment programs and reduced operating budgets by several million dollars. The faculty conducted a vote of no confidence to which the board failed to respond. The president's first year ended with a tense graduation ceremony but no further open conflict. Enrollment at the beginning of the second year was a surprise. The once-growing student body declined by 2 percent. Ten faculty left for other positions. The second year opened calmly. The president hired instructors to replace the departed faculty and indicated he had no intention of filling the vacancies with permanent individuals holding doctoral degrees. The third year brought an alarming decrease in enrollment—5 percent. Private institutions are heavily dependent on tuition, and a total decrease in revenues of 7 percent contributed to serious financial problems. At the beginning of year three, the board asked us to interview campus administration, faculty, and staff to determine the cause of the enrollment decline. What we found was not surprising but illustrative of the damage distrust in identification can do. Faculty and staff told us they were actively advising students to go elsewhere. They believed the long-standing quality of the institution was in jeopardy and students paying over $40,000 per year for tuition were not well served with the current direction. They were no longer proud of their association with the university, and many were actively pursuing other opportunities. Our task was not to determine who was right or wrong, but distrust in identification clearly was taking a severe toll. When we reported our findings to the president and the board, their anger illustrated little willingness to work directly on the issue. Within two more years, the university was forced to layoff over two hundred individuals, student enrollment declined another 6 percent, and donations decreased each year. The president resigned and the board was forced to begin the search process again.

Our university example is not isolated to education. The need for change, the manner of change, resistance to change, and growing distrust must be addressed to avoid the types of problems this example illustrates. Indeed, when distrust in identification becomes severe, organizations may be forced to take actions as extreme as completely rebranding the company to be more palatable to employees and customers. Consider the examples of Andersen Consulting, which changed its name to Accenture after the Enron audit scandal; ValuJet, which became AirTran after a crash in Florida; and Blackwater, the security contractor associated with civilian shootings in Iraq, that changed its name to Xe.[14] The cost of these changes supports the need to understand our identification dimension. Next we talk specifically about building trust for identification.

Building Trust for Identification

"However far the stream flows, it never forgets its source."

—*African saying*

As with our other model dimensions, building trust for identification begins with assessing the current state of identification within the organization and trust levels related to identification. Building a strong identification profile requires communication which trusts employees, customers, and other stakeholders, makes transparent the need for change, and constantly focuses on big-picture and long-term perspectives. Finally, building trust rests with fostering a culture which supports stakeholder identification.

Strategies for Building Trust in Identification

"When you open yourself to trust someone—
identifying with the relationship becomes
more important—we are a low trust culture—
relationships become the control."

—*Anonymous Iranian scientist*

The following strategies, utilized by companies we have worked with over the years, will help your organization to encourage high levels of organizational identification.

Strategy One: Assess Identification and Trust in Identification

Conduct a complete and thoughtful assessment of the current state of identification throughout the organization and the extent to which stakeholders identify with the organization.

Key questions to ask in order to assess identification and trust include:

1. What department and which individuals have the expertise to design a comprehensive assessment? What are the resources needed to support assessment work?
2. Does the organizational culture support identification?
3. Can you identify specific examples of trust in identification? Are there examples of distrust in identification? What can you learn from these examples?

4. What does the organization actively do to help stakeholders experience a connection with the organization?

Strategy Two: Promote Processes and Practices for Identification

Design key processes and practices to support stakeholders identifying with the organization.

Hiring processes should look not only for appropriate technical skills but for a fit between the values of the organization and those of potential employees. Content for employee orientation and training programs should assist employees in connecting their values, needs, and goals to those of the organization. Promotional processes, compensation, and award programs all communicate how employees can or should identify with organizations. Organizational stories, history, celebrations, and use of language support identification. Less visible but equally important are messages of trust and respect for employees as well as tolerance for mistakes. High-identification organizations communicate continually how members of the organization are connected to something special—the core mission of the organization. Customer communication reinforces the desire for identification. Messages about service, problem resolution, quality, and the value of customers all foster identification. Public communication, whether general or to specific audiences, has the opportunity to foster identification through clear statements of values and the special purpose of the organization.

Strategy Three: Communicate for Identification

Excel at communicating stakeholder value, trust, and connection to the organization.

Excelling at stakeholder identification includes designing messages which include explicit statements of how employees and other stakeholders are valued, trusted, and a part of the core of the organization. Messages which help employees believe they are important for the success of the organization, they are a top priority, and they are trusted to do the right thing stimulate identification. Identification messaging to other stakeholders, whether customers, clients, investors, or donors, should stress how the stakeholders are to be treated, the priority they enjoy with the organization, and how loyalty will be rewarded. Loyalty is closely related to identification. Employees and other stakeholders are more loyal to organizations in which communication places a high value on trust. Several research studies support what many practitioners know. Namely, communication that contributes to loyalty and identification incorporates some very basic principles: (1) decisions are explained; (2) communication about change is timely; (3) information flows continuously; (4) change and the impact of change are explained at all organizational levels; and (5) employee and other stakeholder feedback is valued, even when it is not what leaders would have wanted, that is, leaders respond to what is, not what they want to hear.[15]

Excelling at supporting identification requires practicing the art and science of message framing. As Gail Fairhurst explains, "In communication, this implies that the leader is framing a perspective that the direct report does not have, for example, how the tasks within a three-month period fit within the scheme of a yearly plan. The leader's broader perspective provides the potential to shed new light on problems of lesser scope. All other things being equal, perspective adds value and translates to believability."[16] Leadership messages have the potential to provide a big picture and long-term perspective important for stakeholder identification. Framing the future can foster a sense of connection to the special purpose of the organization. Framing the future contributes to sustaining strong stakeholder identification.

Strategy Four: Foster a Culture Supporting Identification

Excel at leading trust building.

Trust is a primary bond in organizations. Importantly, trust building rests with the character and courage of leaders. A culture supporting identification is sustainable only when top leaders understand the importance of trust and genuinely value stakeholder identification. A culture supporting identification is impossible to construct with artificial messages. A culture supporting identification is created through daily practices and policies. It is organizational rhetoric *and* practice. A culture fostering strong identification is characterized by a widely shared vision, with stakeholders understanding the environmental realities of the organization. A strong identification culture lives by visible values and principles broadly familiar across diverse stakeholders. A strong identification culture empowers stakeholders and features collaboration.

The following listing presents questions for building trust in identification.

Questions for Building Trust in Identification
Assess Identification and Trust in Identification

1. How can our organization assess our current identification?
2. Does our culture support identification?
3. Who should be responsible for assessment?

Promote Processes and Practices for Identification

1. Which of our processes and practices should be reviewed to determine their impact on identification?
2. Which of our processes and practices should stay the same?
3. Which of our processes and practices should change? Who is responsible? How can we evaluate the changes for effectiveness?

Communicate for Identification

1. How effectively do we communicate value and respect for stakeholders? What should stay the same? What should change?

2. How effectively does our external communication make clear statements about the values and special purpose of the organization?

3. How effective is our framing of the big picture and long-term perspective for our organization?

Foster a Culture Supporting Identification

1. Do top leaders model trusting and valuing stakeholders?

2. Are organizational rhetoric and practice aligned for identification?

3. Are stakeholders empowered to collaborate with the organization?

Trust in Action: Building a Lasting Culture at IKEA

The IKEA story effectively illustrates what we have been saying in this chapter about the importance of identification and trust in organizations. This remarkable company began in 1943 in the small village of Agunnaryd in Sweden, when its founder Ingvar Kamprad was just seventeen. IKEA is an acronym comprising the initials of the founder's name (Ingvar Kamprad), the farm where he was raised (Elmtaryd), and his home county (Agunnaryd, in Småland, South Sweden). Over six decades, IKEA went from the woods of southern Sweden to becoming a major retailer selling affordable, high-quality home furnishings in thirty-six countries around the world. The IKEA Group now owns 261 IKEA stores in twenty-four countries, with twelve new stores opening in 2009. Thirty-four other stores are owned and run by franchisees in sixteen countries. During a global economic downturn for many retailers, sales for the IKEA Group for 2008 were up by 7 percent to a total of 21.2 billion euro.

This tale of success and continued growth may be due in large measure to the company's culture and values articulated sixty-six years ago by the founder and honored today by IKEA's 127,800 co-workers (not staff or employees—if you work for IKEA, you are a co-worker). Evidence suggests co-workers at all levels of IKEA identify with and feel a strong connection between the organization's vision and their own goals.

We first heard the company's vision described in an interview we conducted with our Italian colleague, Ruggero Cesaria, and IKEA executive Pontus Gabel in November 2008. Gabel is manager of a major change initiative at IKEA. The project's goal is to move the company from a functional to a process-oriented approach for developing new ways to work with suppliers. Speaking with us from Sweden, Gable described reasons for IKEA's success over the years. "Thanks to our co-workers, IKEA provides low-priced furniture with meaning." In the flow of the conversation, Gabel clearly stated IKEA's down-to-earth mission. *"Our vision is to create a better everyday life for the many people.* That is about constantly trying to do everything a little better, a little simpler, even more efficiently, and always cost-effectively. The basic thinking behind all IKEA products is that low prices make well-designed, functional home furnishings available to everyone."

While IKEA's primary vision is to create a better everyday life for the masses, the company also has demonstrated a concern for society and the environment. Before "green" and sustainability were buzzwords in corporate board rooms, IKEA embedded other values related to social and environmental responsibility in its culture, issues related to climate change, preventing abusive child labor, ensuring high-quality working conditions, protecting forestry and wood, and encouraging partnerships and community involvement A case in point is IKEA's community partnership with UNICEF and Save the Children in a Quality Education Soft Toy Campaign. Since 2003, IKEA has been donating one euro for every Soft Toy sold. Soft Toy sales have raised a total of 6.9 million euros, and these donations go to education projects in nine countries.

Co-workers at IKEA support the corporate culture and its values. The company's hiring policy states clearly: "At IKEA, we don't just want to fill vacant jobs; we want to partner with people. We want to recruit unique individuals who share our values. Co-workers are not so restricted at IKEA; we listen and support each individual to identify his or her needs, ambitions, and capabilities. Here are a few examples of our shared values: togetherness, cost-consciousness, respect, and simplicity."

The cultural philosophy articulated in this hiring policy is reinforced by one IKEA co-worker. Edoardo is a customer services and local marketing manager at IKEA in Milan, Italy. He had grown tired of the corporate culture in his previous marketing and communications role, where he felt there was little interest in employees' opinions. According to Edoardo, "At IKEA everyone is treated as an individual. A lot of people are involved in the decision-making process. Everyone's opinion is valued. I am proud to be a part of IKEA. I love the culture and I am a firm believer in the way we work. I would recommend it to anyone I know."

Pontus Gabel told us one last story about identification with IKEA: "If you do something that is not in line with the culture at IKEA, that immediately throws up a stop sign. By contrast, concern and caring for others is always important and is something that comes from the top and from the bottom. All three and a half thousand co-workers here in Sweden attend a Christmas party two days before Christmas, still hosted by IKEA's founder. Each person receives a gift from the founder, and everyone loves it. This event shows you the strong identification we have with the founder. He is eight-two years old, founded IKEA in this small town, and stayed here despite our growth and expansion to many other countries. If I ask people hired from outside IKEA the biggest difference now that they work here, they often say it is the culture and how we care about people."[17]

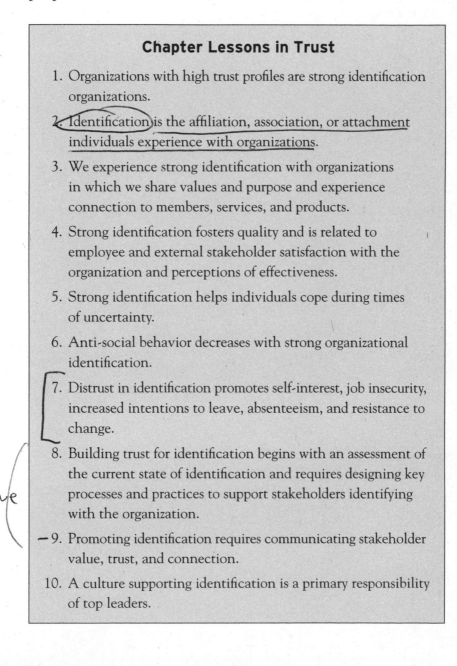

Chapter Lessons in Trust

1. Organizations with high trust profiles are strong identification organizations.

2. Identification is the affiliation, association, or attachment individuals experience with organizations.

3. We experience strong identification with organizations in which we share values and purpose and experience connection to members, services, and products.

4. Strong identification fosters quality and is related to employee and external stakeholder satisfaction with the organization and perceptions of effectiveness.

5. Strong identification helps individuals cope during times of uncertainty.

6. Anti-social behavior decreases with strong organizational identification.

7. Distrust in identification promotes self-interest, job insecurity, increased intentions to leave, absenteeism, and resistance to change.

8. Building trust for identification begins with an assessment of the current state of identification and requires designing key processes and practices to support stakeholders identifying with the organization.

9. Promoting identification requires communicating stakeholder value, trust, and connection.

10. A culture supporting identification is a primary responsibility of top leaders.

Vague

Part Three

CREATING TRUST IN YOUR ORGANIZATION

"We must become the change we want to see in the world."
—*Mahatma Gandhi, civil rights activist, 1869–1948*

In Part Three, we help you create trust in your organization. In the chapters featuring each dimension of our model, we recommended specific strategies for trust building. Part Three explores issues that cut across the five trust dimensions, and we provide tools successfully used by others in trust-building efforts. Here we discuss major challenges for trust: globalization; virtual work environments; innovation, creativity, and risk; conflict and crisis; and building for the future. We provide assessment instruments and processes for you to understand the current state of trust in your organization. We identify specific practices important for trust building. We discuss communication strategies and activities and provide education outlines used successfully by high-trust organizations. These materials are not designed to be prescriptive but are provided to stimulate your planning. They are presented to help you put trust into practice. Trust is the *main thing*, and we want to help you benefit from the results a high-trust organization enjoys.

8

FACING THE CHALLENGES

Trust as Bond and Stimulant

"I think we may safely trust a good deal more than
we do."

—*Henry David Thoreau,*
American Transcendentalist poet, 1817–1862

We have described our trust model with its five no-nonsense
dimensions: competence, openness, concern, reliability, and
identification. We have discussed the benefits of high-trust profiles and described the negatives consequences of distrust. Table 8.1
briefly reviews the findings, which we hope have convinced you:
trust is the main thing.

We are convinced trust is the bond which supports organizations to meet challenges. Trust holds organizations together and
stimulates productive change. High-trust organizations excel,
not because they do not face challenges, but because they lead
with integrity and purpose in pursuit of excellence. High-trust
organizations embrace the future.

Identifying the Challenges

"No one likes having his trust betrayed.
Unfulfilled promises, violations of obligations,
and contractual transgressions hurt, above and
beyond the resources lost."

—*Iris Bohnet, associate professor of public policy*
and the faculty chair of the Women and Public Policy Program at
Harvard University's Kennedy School of Government

Table 8.1 The Organizational Trust Model with Trust and Distrust Outcomes

Trust Model Dimensions	High-Trust Outcomes	Distrust Outcomes
Competence	Good achievement Loyalty Attracts and retains quality employees Increased innovation	Lowered stakeholder loyalty Lowered stakeholder effort and commitment Fear of change
Openness and Honesty	Improved collaboration Reduction of uncertainty	Lowered sharing of information Barriers to innovation
Concern for Employees	High employee satisfaction and retention Productivity goals met Stakeholder loyalty	Stakeholder needs not met Unfair treatment
Reliability	Consistent results Positive perceptions of effectiveness High performance	Abuses of power Broken commitments Lower performance
Identification	Shared values/purpose Promotes positive change Increased quality	Stakeholders pursue self-interests Job insecurity Increased absenteeism and intentions to leave

We live in turbulent times characterized by ongoing change. Few of us have escaped the "work quakes" of the past. Downsizing, reengineering, unprecedented competition, rapidly changing technologies, and globalization are but a few of the factors affecting the vast majority of organizations in both the public and private sectors. Organizational leaders and diverse stakeholders alike have been admonished to examine virtually all taken-for-granted assumptions about organizational functioning. Vision, values, processes, practices, technology, and structures are subject to scrutiny and revision. Trust is the bond and stimulant necessary for productive change during turbulence.[1]

Most agree sophisticated communications technologies will both enable and constrain future organizational practices and processes. Charles Handy, in discussing the evolving virtual organization, describes transitions in a sense of place from the physical to the virtual and identifies challenges associated with eliminating from daily work a physical location and ongoing interpersonal interactions.[2] One of our former clients described his move into a virtual organization with more than 100,000 employees around the globe. Stan Austin had worked for many years in a traditional work environment before moving to a consulting manager role as a "mobilized" employee. In this role, Stan works out of his home or a small regional office about 10 percent of the time and is on the road working on customer projects the other 90 percent of the time. In these projects, Stan works with team members who are located all over the world in such places as China, India, and Mexico. Indeed there are sometimes team members in so many different locations that Stan has to use a computer program to help him identify the best time to hold his virtual meetings (most often conducted by telephone, but occasionally using Skype or the company intranet when there are critical documents or data that need to be shared). To further complicate this "mobilized" environment, the teams Stan works with are project-based, transient teams that form for a short period of time to work a particular customer issue and then disband. Even traditional reporting relationships are different in this environment. As Stan explains, "I was told when I took this job that there would be a good probability that I would never meet my manager face-to-face and so far, a year into this new role, that has been true."

So how does Stan work to build trust in such an environment? "In this environment you have to be really careful how you work with other people because next month they may be leading your project. Things move so quickly you have to be very careful with your relationships. You just don't have the longevity in a relationship if you need to rebuild trust. This is particularly difficult because you have to do all of this without time for team building or access to non-verbal cues in your communication, because most of the interaction occurs on your cell phone or through instant messaging."

Stan's experience is not unusual. Technologies make possible new notions of multinational organizations working with a variety of forms of relationships throughout the globe. Extensive geographic distances, asynchronicity across time zones, and diverse national and regional cultures are important challenges for trust and communication, given the increased spans of global networks. One of the more fundamental challenges for leadership rests with creating the values, attitudes, and behaviors for information sharing. In the past, organizations have been structured to protect and control information. Individuals were seen as owners of information and information ownership was equated to degrees of organizational power. Individual leaders were rewarded for what they knew that others did not. Leadership is challenged to balance between technology and face-to-face interaction. The load of communication increases as the twenty-four-hour work day becomes a reality. Leaders must learn to work with individuals and groups they rarely, if ever, see. Traditional leadership controls are replaced by trusting employees—the imperative of the future.

Organizations must embrace the following challenges to trust: globalization, virtuality, innovation and creativity and risk, and conflict and crisis. Those that actively build trust for the future will thrive. Others will not be as fortunate. It is a conscious choice.

Trust and Globalization

"Though online retailing is evolving at an
unprecedented rate, participants at all levels
still exhibit a fundamental lack of trust."
—*Avinandan Mukherjee and Prithwiraj Nath, business
professors at Montclair State University, New Jersey, and the
University of Nottingham, UK*

Globalization brings to many anxiety, excitement, anxiety, and opportunity. Regardless of the individual or organizational perspective, globalization is one of the challenges most organizations face regardless of size. It is impossible to find clarity in how organizations should adapt to the new realities of a global environment. There are no easy answers. There is no "one right way." Thomas Friedman has coined the depiction, *"the world is flat"* to describe the leveling of the playing field for markets, ideas, influence, and jobs. He concludes:

"The first, and most important, ability you can develop in a flat world is the ability to 'learn how to learn'—to constantly absorb, and teach yourself, new ways of doing old things or new ways of doing new things. This is an ability every worker should cultivate in an age when parts or all of many jobs are constantly going to be exposed to digitization, automation, and outsourcing, and where new jobs, and whole new industries, will be churned up faster and faster. In such a world, it is not only what you know but how you learn that will set you apart. Because what you know today will be out-of-date sooner than you think."[3]

Friedman goes on to claim, "The best companies are the best collaborators. In the flat world, more and more business will be done through collaborations within and between companies, for a very simple reason: The next layers of value creation—whether in technology, marketing, biomedicine, or manufacturing— are becoming so complex that no single firm or department is going to be able to master them alone." And, as we have demonstrated, building trust is fundamental for collaboration.

We recognize the complexity of trust building in global environments with vastly differing cultural perspectives. (This fact is why we developed our model across a variety of cultural contexts.) We have known for a long time there are significant cross-cultural differences in values. Stan Austin described to us some of the challenges in his "mobilized" environment with people from all over the world. "When we are on the road, just finding a suitable place for the team to eat at the end of the day presents a challenge. You have to consider the religious and dietary restrictions of the members of a team, and that can be difficult. All of this is critical in exhibiting concern for the needs of the members of the team."

Cultural differences do impact how individuals approach collaboration. Differences do not, in and of themselves, inhibit collaboration but must be understood for maximum effectiveness. Geert Hofstede has pioneered describing general differences in attitudes and values across cultures. His work, along with that of his colleagues, has become famous for identifying five dimensions of culture that help us understand how differences across cultures (not specific individuals) influence global work. Hofstede's dimensions include: (1) *individualism-collectivism:* refers to the degree members of a culture give precedence to the individual or the group; (2) *power distance:* the degree to which unequal distributions of power and wealth are accepted in a culture; (3) *uncertainty avoidance:* the ways in which different cultures deal with uncertainty about the future and the need for control; (4) *masculinity-femininity:* masculine cultures focus on task achievement and goal orientation, while feminine cultures focus on relationship development, preservation of quality, and harmony; and (5) *Confucian or time-oriented:* refers to long-term or short-term orientation to life and work.[4] We can readily understand how these dimensions influence approaches to collaboration across cultures. Dr. Ruth Ann Lake, author and member of Italian-based Focus Consultants, provided us with an example of what Hofstede describes.

Lake recalled for us, ". . . a recent example of being called in by a pharmaceutical company in southern Spain that had just been acquired by an Indian pharmaceutical company. Right after the acquisition, all managers were fired and a new Indian manager was brought in, purportedly to clean up the company. But this new manager did not speak Spanish and his background in business was in America. He used a U.S. leadership style. His task-oriented approach was top down, not bottom up, and it obviously was not working. He needed to understand the cultural context, not just the language, of the newly acquired company and his personal assignment. It was not a surprise to us that a profound mistrust of the new manager ensued as the remaining Spanish-speaking staff did not understand him, neither his language nor his way of working with people. Most importantly, for them, he showed no interest in developing relationships, instead he appeared only concerned with tasks. When I [Lake] arrived, I learned several managers were planning on leaving and establishing their own company. In this situation, I asked myself what could be done to rebuild trust. My consulting colleague and I immediately recommended the new manager needed business coaching and an understanding of Spanish culture with a need to build relationships and show genuine concern for employees. We decided to conduct training courses for the entire staff at which the new manager would not be present except for social encounters associated with the trainings. At those social events, we suggested he engage in relationship-building conversations with his new staff. Over time, the new manager adjusted to the company and the broader culture, and things began to go much better."[5]

Our colleagues in Italy recently completed a large-scale survey of 1,007 individuals in seventeen countries, exploring their perceptions of trust in the organizations where they work.[6] We took a closer look at the 766 responses from five countries with the most survey respondents: Germany, Italy, Netherlands, United Kingdom, and United States. Our colleagues had asked two questions: "In your experience, what do people from your country of origin require most of all to trust colleagues in a work project?" and "In your experience, what do leaders in your country of origin need to do to gain your trust?" Figure 8.1 presents the results based on our five dimensions of trust. For the question concerning trust in peers, note the emphasis on openness and honesty and reliability. Also note the differences among the countries. For trust in leadership, the pattern changes to combine openness and honesty with concern for employees and competence. Again, note the differences across the five countries. These data help us understand the subtle but important differences Hofstede describes. We don't present the Hofstede dimensions as a full description of cultural differences or the only ones of importance. We present them to stimulate your thinking about the global relationships you form and what differences will be important for your planning. Indeed, a key competency for our global environment may be our abilities to think comprehensively about our circumstances with an emphasis on understanding differences in order to build trust.

As important as they are, cultural value differences are not the only considerations when thinking about trust building in the global environment. When we forge agreements with organizations in other countries, we are influenced by broad national perceptions of trust, financial market conditions, and some fairly specific institutional considerations. In other words, trust in inter-organizational or multi-organizational arrangements relates to trust in governments to honor multi-national agreements; to legal protection of money flows, investments, and intellectual property agreements; and to confidence in institutional operations not dependent on personal familiarity or similarity. In many circumstances, this operational context becomes the first significant determinant for trust.[7] When trust in the operational context is developed, trust based on familiarity and similarity can follow. Recent research focusing on trust in global electronic transactions (e-business, etc.) identifies that for the trillions (yes, trillions) of transactions occurring each year, trust in institutions and electronic platforms is more important than familiarity or similarity with specific individuals supporting the

Figure 8.1 Results of European Responses to Five Trust Dimensions

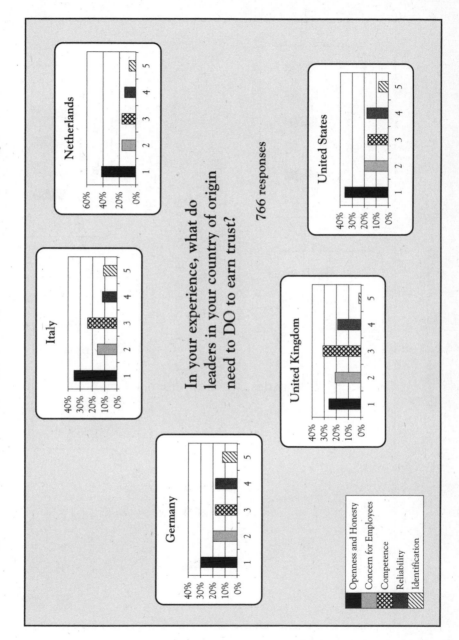

In your experience, what do leaders in your country of origin need to DO to earn trust?

766 responses

Figure 8.1 (*Continued*)

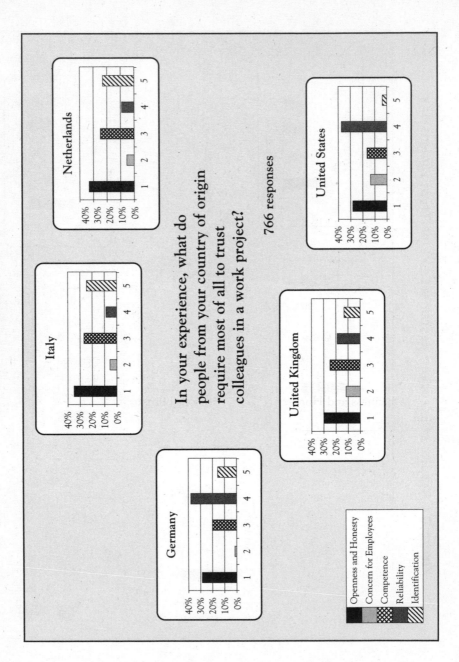

In your experience, what do people from your country of origin require most of all to trust colleagues in a work project?

766 responses

transactions.[8] This is not surprising and it is the future. When thinking about building trust for global partnerships, agreements, or alliances, we must consider how our organizations as institutions within a broader society with specific regulations can assess trust in others and build trust for new relationships. This requires new leadership thinking and new communication strategies. Table 8.2 maps each dimension of our trust model to important institution-based characteristics necessary for trust.

With the challenges of the global environment, it is often difficult to understand where to begin in thinking about trust building. Table 8.3 is a checklist for planning that we have successfully utilized with our clients. We offer it to stimulate your thinking.

Table 8.2 The Trust Model and Institution-Based Trust

Trust Model Dimensions	Institution-Based Characteristics*
Competence	Competence/quality
	Financial balance
	Availability of human resources
	Business practice transfer
Openness and Honesty	Responsibility to inform
	Interaction courtesy
	Feedback mechanisms
Concern for Employees	Procedural fairness
	Cooperative norms
Reliability	Legal compliance
	Lawful contracts
	Fair government regulations
	Appropriate rules and standards
	Assurance of fulfillment of expectations
Identification	Perceived organizational effectiveness
	Perceived credibility
	Perceived risk reduction
	Perceived desire to continue association

*These institution-based characteristics were selected from recent research findings cited in the end notes for this chapter.

Table 8.3 Building Trust in a Culturally Diverse Global Environment: Core Strategies and Questions to Ask*

Core Strategies	Questions to Ask
Study trust in the cultures, countries, or organizations where you will be working.	How do the people in that culture think about what it means to trust someone?
	What is needed to be trusted there in a business transaction?
	Which of the five drivers of trust most affects trust in that culture? Competence, openness and honesty, concern for employees, reliability, or identification?
Become well aware of your own cultural values, concepts, and behaviors about trust.	How does your approach to trust affect your own communication style, behaviors, and attitudes toward others you think are unlike you?
	If there are any differences in trust building attitudes and behaviors based on culture, how can you help bridge the differences?
Don't assume trust is built and maintained and repaired similarly across cultures.	Are you able to identify (and respect) any different approaches to building trust linked to personal, organizational, or cultural values?
	Are the people you are working with demonstrating trust-building behaviors different from yours, perhaps typical of a high- or low-trust culture?
	How can you accommodate or adapt your trust building behaviors to those in the other culture or subcultures?
Create opportunities for global or multi-cultural teams to discuss and define trust.	How can you facilitate a productive dialogue about trust?
	How is trust or its lack affecting work or a work project in the multi-cultural team?
	What does everybody want or need from the team in order to give and get trust?

Table 8.3 (*Continued*)

Core Strategies	Questions to Ask
Go beyond just tolerating cultural differences about trust and learn to value them.	How can discussing differences about trust bring members of a multi-cultural team closer together as a work group with a greater value of trusting relationships? How can a dialogue about trust encourage more creativity and productivity in the team?
Realize that no one single key exists for building trust in all cross-cultural situations and organizations all of the time.	Are you and others you work with able to work productively in an organizational reality that continues to differ in how people approach trust? Are you able to engage in trust-building behaviors and come to trust others in new and innovative ways despite cultural differences?

*Editorial assistance provided by Marianna Amy Crestani, multi-cultural communication consultant

Trust and the Virtual Organization

Over 80 percent of all organizations report significant aspects of their work are performed virtually. Most interact with customers, investors, clients, or donors through electronic communications. Face-to-face familiarity decreases with the increased capability of working across time and space. Leaders are responsible for people they have never met in person. Diverse cultural backgrounds and languages are represented in many teams of workers who support products and services throughout the globe. Physical space is less important than technological connectivity. Work can be performed anywhere, any time, and by anyone (almost). Old control and monitoring systems are obsolete. Charles Handy, mentioned earlier, sums it up in response to a common employee lament, "If they don't trust me, why should

I bother to put their needs before mine?" If it is even partly true that a lack of trust makes employees untrustworthy, it does not bode well for the future of virtuality in organizations. If we are to enjoy the efficiencies and other benefits of the virtual organization, we will have to rediscover how to run organizations based more on trust than on control. Virtuality requires trust to make it work: Technology on its own is not enough."[9]

So what does it take to build trust in virtual organizations? Fortunately, the answers are not different from what we have been proposing in our model. Leaders need to take responsibility for trust building and align strategies with the overall goals and purpose of the organization. We do believe trust building in virtual environments requires a melding of roles and expectations with appropriate technology to support excellent results. The following recommendations are research based and have been tested with clients in a variety of virtual environments.

1. Develop norms and expectations for virtual work. Relate expectations to the vision and purpose of the organization.

2. Set meeting and communication standards.

3. Ensure appropriate skills for using technology (includes employees and other stakeholders).

4. Research and design user-friendly work environments (equipment, supplies, technology, and ergonomic work features, etc.).

5. Use multiple methods of communicating including voice and face-to-face meetings.

6. Ensure employees and other stakeholders know how their work/interaction relates to the overall excellence of the organization.

7. Provide information on individual and organizational results.

8. Ask for feedback and suggestions for improvements.

9. Deal directly and swiftly with trust breaches.

10. Support continual learning and development.

11. Make personal contacts with virtual workers.

12. Reward and recognize contributions.

Building trust in virtual environments through the use of social media is becoming increasingly important. Twitter, Facebook, YouTube, and blogging are only some of the media currently utilized by organizations to create relationships important for trust. The personal expression potential inherent in these media provides opportunities to build trust for individuals who rarely if ever have the opportunity to work face-to-face. However, social media also are subject to the same breaches of trust common among other media. As social media uses increase, leaders and professional communicators informed by employee and other stakeholder needs and preferences must explore how both older and new media work together to influence diverse organizational outcomes.

Trust and Innovation, Creativity, and Risk

"Few things can help an individual more than to place responsibility on him (or her), and to let him know that you trust him."

—Booker T. Washington, former slave and civil rights activist, 1856–1915

"It is simple, if you don't trust me, I will withhold my creativity, I won't be innovative, and I won't risk more than I must. And what is even more important, you won't know that I am withholding because I won't tell you." These are tough statements. But we know they are true. We also know organizations need innovation, creativity, and risk takers more than ever. The global, virtual environment demands it, and we know from personal experience we can't achieve it by ourselves.

Jim Collins, in his bestseller *Good to Great,* claims good is the enemy of great. He writes, "We don't have great schools, principally because we have good schools. We don't have great government, principally because we have good government. Few people attain great lives, in large part because it is just so easy to settle for a good life. The vast majority of companies never become great, precisely because the vast majority become quite good—and that is their main problem."[10] We think this issue of good as the enemy of great applies directly to stimulating innovation, creativity, and risk taking. It is easier to maintain the status quo when things are going relatively well than to face the need to change for the future. We claim we don't, but many still cling to the tried-and-true admonition, "If it isn't broken, don't fix it." We don't trust in change and do not build trust in others important to encourage change. It is sad but true that organizations in crisis can change more rapidly than organizations faced with challenges but still producing relatively good results. However, when challenges are not addressed, storm clouds build and crises follow.

Trust is fundamental to stimulate innovation, creativity, and risk taking. Employees who innovate work in environments that are safe for challenging and changing the status quo. Mistakes are expected and supported when reaching for new solutions. A Hewlett-Packard research and development manager once told us, "If you are always successful, you are not working on exciting problems." He is right. High-trust organizations are more creative, innovative, and able to engage in productive risk taking.

One of the most innovative companies in the world is 3M. Innovation has been essential to the company's success since its earliest days. 3M started when a group of investors bought a piece of land so they could mine corundum, the abrasive that makes sandpaper scratchy. When the investors discovered the land didn't hold any corundum, they had to create new products or quit. The firm's first successful inventions were an abrasive cloth for metal finishing and waterproof sandpaper used for polishing exterior auto finishes. From the outset, innovators at 3M learned from their mistakes. Early inventor Francis Okie initially suggested that sandpaper could be sold to men as a replacement for razor blades. Despite this dubious suggestion, Okie kept his job and went on to invent the waterproof sandpaper that helped the company survive. Today, 3M is a $23-billion manufacturing company with over 70,000 employees worldwide and more than 60,000 products, including Post-it Notes, Scotchgard fabric protector, overhead projectors, heart-lung machines, insulating materials, and light fixtures. Innovation is so important at 3M that it is central to the company's vision—*to be the most innovative company in the markets it serves*.

How does a company as diverse as 3M maintain its creative edge? 3M invests in innovation. To support creativity, current CEO George Buckley increased the R&D budget 20 percent—to a total of $1.5 billion. Further, most successful creators have a sponsor in upper management. Senior executives must be willing to help innovators gain access to resources and offer protection when projects fail. Employees at 3M are trusted to do the right thing. Creative staff at 3M are encouraged to spend up to 15 percent of their time on projects of their own choosing. Known as "bootlegging," this concept enables innovators to work on pet projects without first gaining management approval. Failure is a major concern for innovators, since it will happen to most of them at one time or another. 3M is very insightful in realizing nothing inhibits creativity like the fear of punishment for failure. More than 60 percent of new product ideas developed at 3M ultimately fail. This figure does not include the countless failures occurring on a daily basis in 3M research and development labs. However, successes like the Post-it Note more than compensate for 3M's product failures. Post-its were developed by adapting materials from a failed venture. The compound used for the adhesive on the back of the Post-it Note was initially deemed useless because of its limited adherence to other objects—the very quality that made Post-it Notes a success! Today, there are more than four hundred Post-it products sold in over one hundred countries around the world, and a product born from failure is the centerpiece of 3M's $3.2-billion business products division. Finally, when a product is successful, leaders at 3M recognize those responsible. The Carlton Society, a company hall of fame, honors the achievements of outstanding scientists; the Golden Step Award honors teams of people who have successfully developed and marketed new products. This recognition reinforces the value of innovation and the trust 3M has in its employees.[11]

High-trust organizations are more creative, innovative, and able to engage in productive risk taking. The turbulence in the newspaper industry provides an excellent example. Newspapers today are challenged by all forms of electronic media and fierce competition for advertisers. As president and chief operating officer of *The New York Times* regional media group, Mary Jacobus led a group of fifteen regional newspapers with what observers characterized as an unusually high level of trust. Jacobus described for us the Publishers Innovation Project developed and executed by her team in the beginning of 2008. In this initiative, each of Jacobus' publishers took a segment of the business and built its own team to deliver on a year-long project to make recommendations for change in different areas of business operation. Jacobus asked her publishers to identify areas of interest and to let her know where they felt passionate about driving change. This was the first time Jacobus asked her publishers to work across their newspapers, as contrasted to dealing with local concerns. The initiative was designed to drive change throughout the region. A stunning success was spearheaded by the publisher of the newspaper in Tuscaloosa, Alabama, who had a passion to explore how newspapers in Jacobus' region produced advertising. Working closely with other publishers involved in the Publishers Innovation Project, the team helped to launch a Creative Services Center in Tuscaloosa to produce virtually all of the advertising (95 percent) for the fifteen newspapers. Jacobus approved a significant investment in technology to enable ad copy from all of the newspapers to flow to Tuscaloosa for production and then return to the local papers. The result, according to Jacobus, was a "significant savings" with improved efficiency because successful ads were now broadly shared. As Jacobus explained to us, "If a banner works for a jeweler in Sarasota, we can now utilize the same banner graphics for a jeweler in Tuscaloosa." These publishers are now working to centrally produce magazine copy for the region. Jacobus told us this success came from trusting her publishers to develop creative solutions to problems. Jacobus concluded, "A lot of newspapers are now shipping their advertising copy off to India, so I asked my publishers to look at that option and see whether it made sense for us. The people who work for me came back after a lot of investigation and said we can ship our ads to India, but we think we can do it for about the same price in Tuscaloosa using the creative talent from the design center at the University of Alabama and not only get efficiency, but also get better quality than the work being done in India." The results have been stunning, and now other media organizations are studying what the publishers are doing in Tuscaloosa with hopes of establishing their own creative services centers.[12]

Planned change is more effective in high-trust organizations. Whether structural, technological, or behavioral, effective change is based on trust in decision-makers; openness of information about rationale for change, its impact, and expected results; excellent execution of change (competence); and continuous evaluation of results. The communication strategy and plan for change are a shared responsibility of leaders and communication professionals. The following list provides a series of questions important for developing a high-trust communication strategy and plan in support of change.[13]

Questions to Develop High-Trust Communication
Strategies and Plans for Change
Communication Strategy

1. How should we explain the change?
2. How should we gather input about the change?
3. What do we know about the acceptance or rejection of the planned change?
4. How should we disseminate change outcomes?
5. What approaches should be used for understanding the various audiences for our messages?
6. What are our goals? What are the probable reactions?
7. Which of the following models should we use?

   - Equal dissemination—all stakeholders receive the same information with the same timing sequences.
   - Need to share—all stakeholders receive the same information and all are asked for input.
   - Quid pro quo—giving preferential communication access about change to those who provide something the organization desires, such as money, expertise, approval, power, or other resources.
   - Need to know—information provided only to those who must have information about change or those who have expressly requested information.
   - Marketing method—developing messages for specific stakeholder groups with an emphasis on the particular perspective of a given group.
   - Reactionary method—provides communication only when required by circumstances or events.

8. How can we communicate trust in our strategy?

Communication Plan

1. What messages should be crafted in support of our strategy?
2. Which messages will solicit input?

3. Which messages will provide information?

4. What does analysis of our stakeholders reveal with regard to our messages?

5. Which communication channels should we use?

6. What is the timing for message dissemination?

7. What is our timing for continuing input?

8. How are we going to monitor acceptance or resistance to change?

9. How are we going to know when we need to adjust the plan?

10. What results are we going to communicate? How? To whom? When?

Trust and Conflict/Crisis

"It is essential to employ, trust, and reward those whose perspective, ability, and judgment are radically different from yours. It is also rare, for it requires uncommon humility, tolerance, and wisdom."

—Dee Hock, founder and former CEO of VISA

The words "conflict" and "crisis" are loaded ones. Their definitions depend on the perspectives of individuals, and they often differ. It is the case that "We know conflict or crisis when we see it or experience it." Despite differing perspectives, most agree that trust is fundamental for productive conflict or crisis response. Most also agree conflict and crisis are an inevitable part of organizational life. When we work with our clients to improve their conflict outcomes, we generally describe *conflict* as the processes that occur when individuals, groups, or the entire organization perceives or experiences frustration in attaining goals and addressing issues of concern. *Crisis* is a severe threat to individuals or organizations during which the very continuation of the system or structure of relationships is in question.

Conflict occurs during crisis, conflict can contribute to crisis, but conflict and crisis are not the same processes or experiences.

Research and practical experience both tell us that trust during conflict improves outcomes. When top management teams are in conflict, trust has been demonstrated to provide the glue important for productive resolution. We know leaders make better decisions when differing perspectives and conflicting ideas surface. We know decisions are generally better supported when personal attacks are avoided during conflict. But what is important and sometimes illusive is the underlying trust or distrust present in a leadership group which literally shapes the conflict. When trust is low, leaders may silence important disagreements, refuse to agree based on low trust in individuals presenting ideas, or agree but not support key decisions. When trust is low, leaders often engage in resistance behaviors not surfaced in decision meetings. Regardless of the behavior, the results lower decision quality. The same outcomes can be seen when managers work with employees. When employees trust their manager is open and concerned for them, they will be better able to deal with most conflicts.[14]

The choices made during crises will affect organizations for a long time to come. Poor crisis response damages reputations and lowers trust. The greater the magnitude of the crisis and the longer it lasts, the longer stakeholders remember. Stakeholders become angry and distrust increases if the organization denies responsibility or appears to be slow, inaccurate, or self-serving in its actions and responses. Employees, customers, clients, investors, and donors make decisions about continued relationships with organizations based on how the crisis is handled and how much trust is retained for the organization.[15] When crises are handled using the principles of our trust model, the potential for positive outcomes increases.

Building trust to sustain organizations during crisis begins long before the crisis occurs. Leaders cannot decide they want to be trusted during a crisis when they have given little previous thought to trust building. However, specific actions can be identified which are important for the ability to maintain trust during crises. The first action is the development of a crisis management plan. The list below outlines the basics of a crisis management plan which supports trust building. Once the plan is developed, regular practice of the plan is recommended, including the use of complex simulations. The plan should be periodically reviewed and revised. Crisis leaders should be aware different stakeholders may require different crisis strategies. Employees, shareholders, and customers will probably be affected differently, and their needs and expectations will vary. These considerations should be taken into account when developing crisis plans and responses during crises.[16]

Developing a High-Trust Crisis Management Plan

1. Develop a statement of the principles (or approach) to be applied in dealing with a crisis.

2. Develop a comprehensive list of the most probable kinds of crises for your organization.

3. Form a crisis team (generally, a senior leader heads the team, with members representing specialty areas of communications, legal, human resources, medical, research, operations, technology, safety, security, transportation, and government affairs).

4. Establish a crisis center equipped with communications technology and other materials or supplies to assist in managing crisis response and communication.

5. Develop a list of key stakeholders, including adversaries, and an assessment of each.

6. Create an analysis of resources needed to manage a potential crisis.

7. Develop a statement of media guidelines and suggestions for public communication.

8. Prepare background information on the organization and its policies.

9. Establish an alert system that establishes communication with stakeholders concerning potential problems and, when possible, proposes actions to avert crises.

By now it is clear that communication planning is critical to building and maintaining trust. Communication practices during crisis are pivotal to high-trust organizations. Matthew Seeger's report of the findings of a panel of crisis communication experts helps us think about how to prepare for this important communication responsibility.[17] We have provided—for each of the ten best practices Seeger identifies—the dimension or dimensions of our trust model the practice exemplifies. It becomes readily apparent that thinking about trust during crisis is fundamental for success. The list below summaries the Seeger report identifying each of our trust dimensions.

Best Practices for High-Trust Crisis Communication

1. Make risk and crisis communication part of the decision process itself. Communications should not merely be involved in communicating decisions about risk and crisis after they have been made. (*Competence*)

2. Identify risk areas and corresponding risk reduction, preset initial crisis responses so that decision making during a crisis is more efficient, and identify necessary response resources. (*Competence*)

3. Ongoing efforts should be made to inform and educate the public using science-based risk assessments. During a crisis, the public should be told what is happening, and organizations managing crises have a responsibility to share this information. (*Openness and honesty*)

4. Respond quickly through social media channels with authentic communication. Apologize quickly and sincerely when mistakes have been made. (*Openness and honesty*)

5. Listen to the public's concerns and understand the audience. Take the public's concerns into account and respond to them accordingly. (*Concern and identification*)

6. Be honest and open. Honesty is necessary to build credibility and trust before and during a crisis. Openness about risks may promote an environment of risk sharing. If information about a crisis is not shared openly by the organization engaged in the crisis, the public will obtain information from other sources. (*Openness and honesty*)

7. Collaborate and coordinate with credible sources. Develop a pre-crisis network to coordinate and collaborate with other credible sources. Coordinating messages enhances the probability of consistency and may reduce public confusion. (*Openness and honesty, reliability, competence*)

8. Meet the needs of the media and remain accessible. The media are a primary conduit to stakeholders. Crisis communicators should view the media as strategic resource to aid in managing the crisis. (*Openness and honesty*)

9. Communicate with compassion, concern, and empathy. Designated spokespersons should demonstrate appropriate levels of compassion, concern, and empathy. (*Concern*)

10. Accept uncertainty and ambiguity. Risks always include some level of uncertainty. Crises and disasters are by definition abnormal, dynamic, and unpredictable. (*Competence*)

11. Use messages of self-efficacy. Messages of self-efficacy are most effective when they recommend a range of specific harm-reducing actions to those affected by the crisis, focusing on what can be done to help others. Messages of self-efficacy need to be constructed carefully so that the reason

for the action is clear, consistent, and meaningful. (*Concern, Identification*)

Ray Gomez, a risk and crisis communication consultant working with leading global organizations, sums up the critical nature of trust during crisis, "Most crises are not accidents; they are the result of bad management. [Referring to the financial crisis beginning in 2008.] For example, an insidious process of bad governance in many financial organizations over at least the last fifteen years resulted ultimately in the current financial crisis. The lending industry, insurance companies, and the real-estate industry have allowed bad practices to become accepted practices. To rebuild trust in a crisis like this, organizations need to start at the top and set a tone which articulates they have learned their lessons. Business practices must become more transparent, ethical, and sound."[18] Gomez underscores what we have been claiming about trust and conflict and crisis.

Trust and the Future

"Before I can live with other folks, I've got to live with myself. The one thing that doesn't abide by majority rules is a person's conscience."
—Harper Lee, 1961 Pulitzer Prize–winning author

We have focused on the importance of building trust and repairing breaches of trust. We now want to focus on building trust for the future of your organization. Most acknowledge fast-paced change is the order of the day and a fundamental leadership challenge. However, many of us get caught in the trap of responding to the tyranny of the urgent without focusing on the importance of building for the future.

Leadership roles are rapidly changing requiring increased communication expertise. Visionary thinking and analytical skills remain important; however, leaders succeed in producing outstanding results only when they are trusted by their constituents to make changes during uncertainty and lead for a better future.

Increasingly, organizations of the twenty-first century are described as borderless and boundaryless. The "middle-less" organization gains attention as a new organizational design. Fewer managers with larger spans of control are found in almost all types of organizations. Work teams are given higher degrees of autonomy and control over immediate work situations. The goals are to increase performance and improve overall morale. The traditional responsibilities of managers are replaced as power and control are passed to diverse levels in the organization. Managers become facilitators, coaches, teachers, and experts, whereas previously they may have been controllers, directors, planners, and rewarders. The new responsibilities are roles, not new organizational positions. The new responsibilities require sophisticated communication competencies. Advances in technology give rise to the concept of networked teams; leaders and managers must learn how to contribute to teams of people who may not be in the same geographic location and only work face-to-face on rare occasions if at all.[19]

Professional communicators have increased responsibility. Developing formal communication policy increasingly is the responsibility of professional communicators in collaboration with top leaders. Policy guides action, holds leaders accountable, and requires implementation strategies, which include message development, dissemination, feedback, and evaluation. The spin doctors of the past are replaced with professionals who understand data collection and interpretation, who understand the needs of diverse stakeholders, who develop credible message strategies, who utilize diverse technologies wisely, and who understand the demands of an *instant information, virtual* world. Angelique Rewers, president and owner of Bon Mot Communications, describes what she considers the most important challenges for professional communicators in today's environment. Rewers believes, "The low trust paradigm is inextricably linked to the social media phenomenon because the proliferation of social media has empowered a multitude of stakeholders to share information freely. The consequence of this radically democratized ability for individuals to create, disseminate, and consume information—combined with dwindling trust in organizations (both internally and externally)—is unprecedented transparency into organizations' internal and external actions and communications. Thanks to social media, organizations can no longer 'control the message' or segment audiences. Rather, what an organization says or how an organization treats one group of stakeholders is readily apparent to all other stakeholders. Therefore, if a corporation breaches trust with its employees, the ripple effects spill over into the organization's relationship with customers. If a company betrays its customers or investors, the impact affects the way it is treated by regulators. Both executives and communicators need to understand and appreciate the link between social media and organizational trust." Rewers continues, "Many companies have yet to adjust their communications strategies to take into account the varying needs, likes, and dislikes of the different generations within their organizations. However, the manner or channel often makes a significant difference in how much trust people have in particular information. While older Baby Boomers may not feel as though blogs are 'real news,' Millenials may see these sources as more trustworthy because they are from 'real people' instead of 'the establishment.' Some employees may be more accustomed to and feel more comfortable with face-to-face meetings. On the other hand, younger workers often feel their time is wasted in meetings when they could have just as easily received the information via email or text. Moreover, those same employees may find restrictions on texting, instant messaging, visiting social media/networking sites and blogging as a breach of the organization's trust in them."[20] To support excellence, communication professionals of today and tomorrow must have an understanding of trust building and trust repair that incorporates an understanding of social media such as blogs, wikis, and social networking sites (SNS). Social media can be effective as proactive tools for building trust. CEO and employee blogs and SNS accounts provide a means for organizations to build relationships. But these relationships will be positive only if interactions are authentic. Blogs, status updates, and tweets should be developed with an emphasis on sincerity, openness and honestly, genuine concern for others, and an awareness of legal issues.

Chapter Lessons in Trust

1. Trust building is complicated by the global environment.

2. Cultural differences influence but do not have to inhibit collaboration.

3. Trust in global alliances is influenced by trust in governments, legal protections, and institutional operations not dependent on personal familiarity or similarity.

4. For global alliances, institution-based trust usually precedes relationship trust.

5. Trust is the core of making a virtual work environment productive.

6. Trust is fundamental to stimulate innovation, creativity, and risk taking.

7. Planned change is most effective in high-trust organizations.

8. Trust improves conflict outcomes.

9. Organizational choices during crisis affect long-term organizational success.

10. Leaders and professional communicators share responsibility for building trust in an organization's future.

9

BUILDING TRUST

"The capacity to engage in effective and
comprehensive trust building is critical to
organization success in the complex, competitive,
and technologically mediated global economy of
the 21st century."

—Anonymous leader in
multi-national corporation

Building and rebuilding organizational trust are based on action more than on good intention. One of our clients recently told us, "Most of us here have good intentions with regard to trust, but fewer of us translate those intentions into strategic action." Many leaders could have made this statement. We know from experience leaders frequently become so busy with daily challenges they simply do not pay strategic attention to the very actions that could transform their organizations as well as elevate their leadership effectiveness. We do believe most leaders have excellent intentions. We want to conclude this book with merging intentions into actions—actions designed to directly address distrust, increase trust, and produce results.

Understanding Distrust

Many of us can readily identify distrust stemming from a serious violation of expectations, an integrity breach, illegal behavior, or other unethical behaviors. Fewer of us notice the beginnings of gradual erosions of trust within our organizations. Regardless of how it begins, distrust fosters reactions important for all types of organizational relationships and outcomes.

When distrust is present, individuals—and sometimes the entire organization—seek to determine the seriousness of the violation(s), assign responsibility, and assess the severity of the impact. These assessments rarely are based on factual understanding alone. Emotional reactions to distrust vary ranging from ambivalence, hurt, and anger to, in some cases, the permanent fracturing of relationships. When distrust is evidenced, leaders must first determine how pervasive the distrusting reactions are. What are the causes? And finally, how can distrust be overcome? Distrust does not go away because we want it to disappear. Distrust must be approached with intentional action addressing the causes of distrust and making visible corrective strategies for regaining trust.

While there are endless reasons for distrust, we think the four most common are (1) big mistakes whether in strategy or quality; (2) major changes such as mergers, global sourcing, downsizing, and restructuring; (3) ethical violations; and (4) highly political environments. An awareness of these four can help us understand the dynamics of distrust and identify actions dedicated to overcoming distrust.

Mistakes in strategy occur in most organizations. We do not operate with a clear, unencumbered view of tomorrow. Mistakes can be costly and, at best, lower trust in the competence of leadership and, at the worst, generate outright distrust. One of our clients described to us the hostility and distrust that resulted from the announcement that their newest plant (in operation only eighteen months) would be closed and sold to a competitor. Over five hundred employees had relocated to be a part of what they thought was an important technology for their organization's future. Leaders stated directly they believed it was a strategic mistake to continue to pursue the technology in question, based on current market positioning and the organization's strengths in other areas. Although most of the affected employees were offered jobs elsewhere, our client reported, "Employees did not buy we had made a strategic mistake. Many believed we had sold out for short-term gains and were undermining years of planning for the new facility, not to mention showing no regard for the disruption to their lives and the lives of their families. Some of our most promising engineers left the organization and went to work for our competitors." It is difficult to determine in this case whether the "strategic mistake" was building or selling the plant. What is not in question was the cost to our client of the loss of important talent based on distrust of leadership decision making.

Change of any type almost always has the potential to generate distrust. In recent years, the major change that downsizing brings has occurred in many sectors, whether resulting from mergers, global sourcing, financial crises, restructuring, or a host of other market conditions. In general, research supports the negative impact on trust that occurs during downsizing, even for those who remain with the organization.[1] Downsizing frequently results in lowered productivity, lowered commitment, withholding of creativity, and a host of other problems, ranging from perceptions of injustice to declines in both mental and physical health of employees. Not surprisingly, employees with the least information about the decisions to be made react the most negatively. The issue is not whether downsizing should or should not occur; the issue is about trust and distrust during change and how the major outcomes of change are related to trust.

We have talked about the continuing global financial crisis, with its host of ethical violations, as one of the most visible examples in recent history of fear replacing trust and literally generating the collapse of organizations, impacting the future of hundreds of thousands of individuals. As bad as the financial crisis is, ethical violations of lesser visibility occur daily in many organizations. Individuals are treated unfairly, fraud occurs, problems are ignored, betrayal happens, people get even with each other, mistakes are covered up, and sabotage undermines excellence. Depending on the visibility and pervasiveness of these violations, distrust builds rapidly or sometimes very slowly. Either way, distrust builds with a direct, negative impact on excellence.

As most would agree, the political environment of many organizations contributes to levels of distrust—often among top leaders. Gamesmanship, taking individual credit, blaming, and a host of self-promoting behaviors are associated with the politicized environment of moving up the organizational ladder. Creating a "we versus them" competitive mentality between and among groups within organizations is a proven strategy for increasing distrust. Sadly, many believe negative politics are an inevitable part of organizational life. We agree they are a frequent part of organizational life, but reject the notion that we have no choice. We have choices. Actively planning to address distrust is the most important strategy for overcoming the negative impacts of mistakes, major change, ethical violations, political environments, and a host of other distrust producing circumstances.

Overcoming Distrust

Leaders who effectively address distrust do not shield themselves from inconvenient facts. Even when distrust is an unfair reaction to leadership decisions, leaders who are effective work with the reality of the negative in order to stimulate a more productive future. When mistakes have been made, effective leaders take responsibility for mistakes and the problems mistakes generate. Responsibility is blame's positive counterpart. When leaders take responsibility, they are acknowledging problems, accepting the obligation to correct mistakes, and implementing needed change. Effective leaders learn from their own mistakes and are students of the mistakes of others. Effective leaders hold themselves accountable and communicate specific accountabilities across all levels of the organization. Effective leaders, with the assistance of communication professionals, continuously make visible their progress in correcting mistakes and problems.

Leaders cannot avoid making change. In fact, productive change is a core leadership responsibility. However, we have demonstrated the often negative outcomes of major change. Overcoming the distrust of change is based on a commitment to adopting a change management process, which deals with the impact of change in addition to implementing the technical aspects of change. The process described in the list below is the one we have utilized with our clients and is a process associated with productive change in high-trust organizations. We acknowledge there are other effective processes. The primary requirement for overcoming distrust is accepting the fact that productive change is based on more than the technical aspects of moving an organization from one state to another. Overcoming distrust requires an understanding of the impact of change—both negative and positive—for all organizational stakeholders. It requires understanding how the change relates to our five dimensions of trust—competence, openness, concern, reliability, and identification. Finally, it requires setting a vision for change that incorporates inconvenient truths while moving to a better future.

A Process for Making Productive Change and Questions for Change Leaders
Establish a Compelling Vision for the Change

1. Why is the change needed?
2. What are the anticipated results?
3. Who will benefit?
4. What are the potential negatives?
5. Who will be adversely impacted?

Create the Change Leadership Team

1. What expertise is needed for the change effort?
2. Who has the expertise needed for the change?

3. Who specifically should be involved?

4. Can key individuals devote the needed time?

5. Are potential team members credible to stakeholders who are most affected by the potential change?

6. Do team members need education in productive change?

Develop Information Needed to Generate the Change Plan

1. Assess the completeness and accuracy of current data in support of change.

2. Review the completeness and accuracy of data that do not support the change.

3. Identify data gaps and methods to collect missing data.

4. Determine methods to collect information about attitudes toward change from most impacted stakeholders.

Establish the Change Implementation Plan

1. What actions need to be taken?

2. What is the timeline?

3. Who is responsible for each action?

4. What are the resources needed?

5. How does our plan impact perceptions of competency, openness, concern, reliability, and identification?

Establish the Communication Plan

1. Who is responsible for developing the communication plan? Who are the key stakeholders?

2. Which media should be utilized?

3. What are the resources needed?

4. What input and feedback processes should be established?

5. How should the anticipated results be communicated?

6. How should resistance/disagreement/distrust be approached?

7. How does our plan impact perceptions of competency, openness, concern, reliability, and identification?

Implement the Plan

1. How will each action of the plan be monitored?

2. How will the team respond to needed plan changes?

3. Who will review stakeholder input and when?

4. What data will be utilized to determine results?

5. How will changes be communicated?

Evaluate and Communicate the Results

1. Did the process achieve the desired results?

2. If results achieved are excellent, why?

3. If results achieved are not satisfactory, why?

4. How has communication about the results been received?

5. How do the results impact perceptions of competency, openness, concern, reliability, and identification?

Effective leaders respond quickly to ethical abuses. Distrust grows when abuses are ignored, action is delayed, or a veil of secrecy surrounds addressing ethical violations. To be sure, legal actions can constrain what is communicated with respect to correcting certain ethical abuses. However, legal constraints should not block communicating basic action to address known ethical violations. Effective leaders, legal counsel, and communication professionals must work collaboratively to determine how best to communicate in particular circumstances. A core message should make clear that ethical violations will not be tolerated, that a complete understanding of the violating situation will be developed, and that safeguards will be put in place to prevent further abuses.

Tough choices are sometimes necessary to overcome distrust. Serious mistakes, destructive change, ethical violations, or negative political behaviors may require changing leaders or individual contributors. Firing someone should not be a first choice, but in well-understood circumstances should not be the last choice. We can report at least three times in recent years when individuals terminated finally understood the impact of their behaviors and now appear to be more positive contributors than in their previous organizations. We regularly tell our clients what we have continuously said in this book, "Overcoming distrust is not simple or easy; building trust can be difficult and even painful, but it is the main thing leaders can do to promote organizational excellence."

We have spent considerable time in previous chapters talking about tangible and less tangible actions to build trust in competence, openness and honesty, concern for stakeholders, reliability, and identification. Now we are going to identify a series of steps that unite these dimensions and can contribute to excellence in your organization.

We are talking about building a culture of trust, creating a shared vision among stakeholders about a positive present and future, and developing a shared sense of competitive or environmental realities. We are talking about acting in support of values that support trust and aligning operations with these values. We are talking about making trust a powerful force, that is, the *main thing* in your organization, starting by developing your own profile of trust.

Profiling Organizational Trust

Understanding the trust profile of our individual organizations is fundamental to building trust or repairing distrust. By now you know trust is dynamic and changes both slowly and rapidly. We recommend regular trust profiles as one measure for understanding the impact of strategic direction and communication

efforts on trust. On a CD at the end of this book, we have provided the Organizational Trust Index (OTI), a research-based
survey developed with International Association of Business
Communicators (IABC) Research Foundation sponsorship. In
Chapter Two we described the research project from which our
trust model and the survey were developed.

The Organizational Trust Index assists organizations of any
size in understanding the crucial dimensions of trust in particular settings. It provides organizational leaders and communication
professionals an easy-to-administer profile important to support
planning ranging from communication of vision, objectives,
and policies to a variety of major change efforts. The profile can be
of enormous value in the development of education and training
efforts and, when administered regularly, provides tracking data
useful for interpreting organizational actions over time. When
a sample or the entire population of an organization completes
the trust survey, the scores can be compared to the average scores
obtained from organizations, industries, and geographical cultures throughout the world. But more important than broad comparisons, the scores can guide leaders in their understanding of
trust strengths and vulnerabilities at a specific time within a specific organization. The OTI results can assist you in determining
where best to build upon your organization's foundation of trust.
In the CD at the end of this book we have provided a guide for
interpreting your results and communicating those results to others. For many organizations, the OTI has been embedded in regular employee climate and satisfaction surveys. We believe this is
effective, as long as the methodology for administration is sound
and data interpretation appropriate and reliable.

Identifying Productivity Measures
for Trust Monitoring

Regular collection of data profiling organizational trust is insufficient to produce the results most organizations seek. Trust is
fundamental to excellence and is reflected in a very diverse set

of organizational outcomes. The productivity measures to be tracked along with an organization's trust profile are organization-specific and should be selected with care and understanding of the vision and objectives of the specific organization. The selected productivity measures assist an organization in focusing trust-building efforts and also help identify subtle but important shifts in trust over time. We recommend a regular review of productivity measures and trust profile results to assist in strategic planning, education and training, and a wide variety of communication efforts. The following list provides some possible choices for trust monitoring.

Organizational Measures for Monitoring Trust Levels

1. Financial performance
2. Competitive positioning
3. Productivity compared to industry/sector benchmarks
4. Levels of collaboration and cooperation
5. Performance in strategic alliances
6. Flexibility and coordination costs
7. Employee commitment and morale
8. Customer/donor/other stakeholder loyalty
9. Innovation environment
10. Support for change initiatives
11. Leadership effectiveness
12. Productivity in virtual teams
13. Employee turnover rates
14. Employee absenteeism rates
15. Accidents and worker compensation claims
16. Litigation records
17. Ethical/legal abuses

18. Media coverage

19. Crisis management

20. Industry/sector reputation

These are not the only measures an organization can examine. In the above list, we have identified common measures used in trust research and by our clients.[1]

Policies and Procedure Review

A wide variety of organizational policies and practices should be reviewed regularly for how they communicate the trust values of the organization. Generally speaking, the more detailed and prescriptive policies and practices become, the more distrust is communicated to stakeholders. The more policies and procedures empower people to "do what is right," the more trust is supported. We also believe a regular review of policies and operating procedures assists organizations in eliminating redundant directions and creates potential for simplification, leading to increased productivity. We advise revision of any policy or procedure that does not support trust. For example, necessary compliance policies can support trust when they provide a strong rationale for their need and include an emphasis on the equity with which they will be implemented. We have frequently found in our work with clients that it is not the intent of the policy or procedure that creates distrust, but the language of its presentation and the inequity of its implementation. The next list identifies categories of policies and practices where regular review has potential for trust building.

Categories for Policy and Procedure Review

1. Hiring policies and practices

2. Performance feedback and appraisal

3. Compensation policies and practices

4. Disciplinary processes

5. Termination processes and practices

6. Promotional processes and practices

7. Employee benefits

8. Vendor policies and practices

9. Sexual harassment policies and practices

10. Workplace harassment policies and practices

11. Conflict of interest policies and practices

12. Ethical standards

13. Customer/client relationships

14. Confidentiality of private information

15. Financial responsibility

16. Communication of information

17. Feedback processes

18. Media relations

19. Corporate/organizational communication standards and practices

20. Organizational philanthropy

Aligning Vision, Strategic Direction, Operations, and Trust

Leaders should regularly review the organization's vision, strategic direction, and operational plans for trust impact. We recommend at least one leadership team session per quarter devoted to specifically focusing on trust and the realities of the current environment. We know difficult decisions often must be made. We also know too few pay attention to how those decisions can be honestly framed to enhance currency in the trust bank. If a leadership team is not experienced in this type of reflective planning, we recommend finding those either within the organization or from an experienced consultant group who can provide expert facilitation. We have seen in organization after organization results that more than pay for this time and effort. Reflective planning can become a strong component of leadership development. On the CD that accompanies the book, we outline a facilitation approach for this type of session.

Education for Leaders, Supervisiors, Teams, Virtual Environments, and Individual Contributors

We use the word "education," although many would say training and development. We say education because we believe understanding trust requires instilling fundamental concepts that go beyond the skills needed to perform effectively in a given position. Training is important, but educating people throughout the organization about the fundamental concepts of trust has lasting value. If I understand the fundamental concepts related to competence, openness and honesty, concern for others, reliability, and identification, I am able to align a wide range of actions to support trust. I am empowered to become a trust builder. We know from our experiences education about trust can work, regardless of the background of the participants. We believe all executive and supervisory development programs should incorporate education about trust. We also recommend individual contributors receive trust education with a particular emphasis on virtual environments. On the CD, we have provided sample education outlines for executive and supervisor development, individual contributors, teams, and virtual environments.

Developing a Communication Strategy

Throughout this book, we have emphasized that trust is not some ambiguous, illusive concept—it is communication-based.

All behaviors and organizational action are evaluated along trust dimensions, and trust drives behaviors and action. An excellent communication strategy is required for increasing trust and addressing the negative impact of distrust.

The strategy must begin with a solid leadership communication plan. Leaders must put their intentions into messages and actions. Most leaders do not have intuitive or practical experience at crafting the plan. Communication professionals working with leaders should detail the types of messages needed and specifically outline proposed activities in support of a leadership communication strategy. Considerations to include are critical themes; messages desired and needed; media utilized; formal and informal situations; audiences; frequency; and feedback. Many intelligent leaders exhibit only marginal ability to effectively communicate in public settings. Training may be required for communicating directly with a wide variety of stakeholders, including the media. Communication training is viewed by some as insulting, while others know the essence of leadership is linking intelligence and intentions to credible action. What comes out of a leader's mouth is far more telling than what the leader was thinking or intending.

Another critical process for building trust is regular feedback processes from employees and other key stakeholders. Listening should not occur accidentally, or rarely. Excellent communication strategy includes regular and comprehensive employee and stakeholder feedback processes. Communication professionals, along with human resource, marketing, advertising, media, development, and regulatory (finance, legal, etc.) personnel, should carefully design feedback processes appropriate for a specific organization. Additionally, feedback processes must include broad environmental information important for thinking about future issues and needs. Social media should be included in this planning.

Finally, an excellent communication strategy includes the deliberately designed messages to both internal and external audiences. Do these messages build trust or contribute to distrust? How can they be evaluated for their effectiveness? An example from one of our clients helps illustrate. Our client scored relatively high on all of the measures of trust in the OTI except for identification. Interestingly enough, our client was experiencing high turnover among several categories of professionals. We facilitated a review of internal publications over the past two years. What the review discovered was that information about the organization's performance was clearly and reliably presented. However, only two stories about individual employees and their accomplishments had been run. The communications director determined in-house publications had not paid enough attention to linking employees to corporate objectives and illustrating how employees could achieve their individual goals with the organization. Over the next twelve issues of the house magazine, two stories per issue featured teams and individual contributors as they helped the organization meet its objectives. A column on new hires, promotions, and retirements was added. When the employee survey was run the following year (including in this case the OTI measures as it had in the past), identification scores had increased at a statistically significant level. No other specific changes had occurred within the communication strategy.

Finally, one other simple approach is utilized by many of our clients. When internal and external messages are developed, focus groups are asked to evaluate the messages for what they say about competence, openness and honesty, concern for others, reliability, and identification. Not all messages cover all five dimensions all of the time. The real goal is creating a sense of the balance among the five trust dimensions needed in a specific organization.

Final Thoughts: Trust Is the Main Thing

We hope we have made the case: *High organizational trust positively transforms individuals and entire organizations.* Trust building is a primary leadership imperative. Communication professionals are important members of the trust team, helping organizations link intentions, behaviors, and results. Trust is not as some would have us believe—a nice, illusive concept unsuited for a turbulent, uncertain, rapidly changing, and often frightening world. Trust is the bond and stimulant that produces lasting, excellent results. Trust replaces certainty and control as our bridge to the future. Trust stops fear in its tracks. We have choices. The choice to build trust is practical and will bring measurable positive results. The choice to build trust also speaks to the best in all of us, our high ideals, and our dreams for the future. We hope you will lead with trust as the *main thing*.

Endnotes

Preface

1. For a discussion of high-performance organizations and trust, see Covey S.M.R. & Merrill, R.R. (2008). *The speed of trust: The one thing that changes everything.* New York: The Free Press, and Covey, M. (2008). *Trust is a competency. Chief Learning Officer,* 7, 54–56. For specific references to trust and bottom-line performance, see R. Kramer & K. Cook (Eds.). (2004). *Trust and distrust in organizations: Dilemmas and approaches.* New York: Russell Sage Foundation.

Chapter One

1. In this incident, the name, Larry Reynolds, is fictionalized, but the incident is a real one. This convention is followed throughout the book. When a company is not named, the incident or example we describe is real, but we changed the name(s) of the person(s) involved.
2. Gross, D. (2008, October 20). The anatomy of fear. *Newsweek,* pp. 31–33.
3. American Management Association. (1999). Workforce growth slows, AMA's 13th annual workforce survey shows. Available: www.amanet.org.
4. For more information about how violations of trust affect employees and employers, see Braun, C. (1997). Organizational infidelity: How violations of trust affect the

employee-employer relationship. *The Academy of Management Executive, 4,* pp. 11, 94.

5. Jim Paulsen was the keynote speaker at the Southern Colorado Economic Forum presented by the University of Colorado at Colorado Springs on October 10, 2008.

6. Glassner, B. (2000). *The culture of fear: Why Americans are afraid of the wrong things.* New York: Basic Books.

7. Friedman, T. (2008, October 1). Rescue the rescue. *The New York Times,* p. A29. Retrieved November 13, 2008, from http://www.nytimes.com.

8. Niegel Ewington made his remarks during his presentation, "Building a Culture of Trust in Global Emergency Response Teams," SIETAR Congress (Society for International Education, Training, and Research), October 24, 2008.

9. Richard Lowe made his remarks during a workshop, "Speed to Market Trust as a Critical Global Team Factor: A U.S.-Japan Biotech Case Study," SIETAR Congress (Society for International Education, Training, and Research), October 24, 2008.

10. Yang, J., & Salazar, V. (2008, November 20). Most company leaders aren't communicating. *USA Today,* p. 1B.

11. Amendment 47 by Coloradans for Middle Class Relief. (personal communication, October 2008). Quoted from a direct-mail piece published to urge a no vote on Colorado Amendment 47.

12. Abramsky, S. (2008, October 24). The new fear. *The Chronicle Review,* pp. B6–B10.

13. Beckman, H.B., Markakis, K.M., Suchman, A.L., & Frankel, R.M. (1994). The doctor-patient relationship and malpractice. *Archives of Internal Medicine, 154,* 1365–1370; Levenson, W., Roter, D.L., Mullooly, J.P., Dull, V.T., & Frankel, R.M. (1997). Physician-patient communication: The relationship with malpractice claims among primary care physicians and surgeons. *Journal of the American Medical Association, 227*(7), 553–559.

14. The Sarbanes-Oxley Act of 2002 (Pub.L. 107–204, 116 Stat. 745, enacted 2002–07–30), also known as the Public Company Accounting Reform and Investor Protection Act of 2002 and commonly called SOx or Sarbox, is a United States federal law enacted on July 30, 2002, in response to a number of major corporate and accounting scandals, including those affecting Enron, Tyco International, Adelphia, Peregrine Systems, and WorldCom.

15. Severgnini, B. (2006). *La bella figura: A field guide to the Italian mind*. New York: Broadway Books.

16. Byrne, J.A. (2002, July 8). Inside McKinsey: Enron isn't its only client to melt down. Suddenly, times are trying for the world's most prestigious consultant. *BusinessWeek*. Retrieved August 4, 2008, from http://www.businessweek .com; Skapinker, M. (2003, December 29). Seasoned survivor at the head of the firm. *Financial Times*. Retrieved August 4, 2008, from http://www.ft.com.

17. US Airways pilots: We're pressured to cut fuel. (2008, July 17). *USA Today*. Retrieved August 12, 2008, from http:// usatoday.printthis.clickability.com; US Airways pilots: We're pressured to cut fuel. (2008, July 16). *MSNBC*. Retrieved August 12, 2008, from http://www.msnbc.msn.com; Pilots: US Airways pushing to reduce fuel loads to unsafe levels. (2008, July 16). *Fox News*. Retrieved August 12, 2008, from http://www.foxnews.com; Pilots: US Airways pressure to cut fuel unsafe. (2008, July 16). *CBS 5*. Retrieved August 12, 2008, from http://cbs5.com/national/us.airways. pilots.2.772910.html.

18. Sidel, R., Ip, G., Phillips, M.M., & Kelley, K. (2008, March 18). The week that shook Wall Street: Inside the demise of Bear Stearns. *Wall Street Journal*; Story L. (2008, July 12). Regulators seize mortgage lender. *New York Times*. Retrieved February 10, 2009, from http://www.nytimes.com/2008/07/12/ business/12indymac.html. Dash, E., & Sorkin, A.R. (2008, September 25). Government seizes WaMu and sells some

assets. *New York Times*. Retrieved February 10, 2009, from http://www.nytimes.com/2008/09/26/business/26wamu.html.
19. Retrieved February 10, 2009, from http://www.gallup.com/video/111946/Americans-Torn-Support-Auto-Bailout.aspx.
20. Clark, E. (2004). *Around the corporate campfire: How great leaders use stories to inspire success*. Sevierville, TN: Insight; Goldberg, A.B., & Ritter, B. (2006, August 2). Costco CEO finds pro-worker means profitability. *ABC News* online; Greenhouse, S. (2005, July 17). How Costco became the anti-Wal-Mart. *New York Times* online edition; *The Costco Connection* (October 2006 edition).
21. For more information about Costco's approach to higher wages, see http://www.businessweek.com/magazine/content/04_15/b3878084_mz021.htm, retrieved January 2008.
22. For information about Costco's trade in and recycle program, see http://www.greensight.com/CostcoTrades/Common/equiptypes.aspx, retrieved January, 2008.
23. For more information about the value of high levels of trust in various types of organizations, see Argyris, C. (1993). *Knowledge for action: A guide to overcoming barriers to organization change*. San Francisco: Jossey-Bass; Barnes, L.B. (1983, March). Managing the paradox of organizational trust. *Harvard Business Review*, pp. 107–116; Bennis, W., & Bierderman, P.W. (1997). *Organizing genius: The secrets of creative collaboration*. Reading, MA: Addison-Wesley; Brockner, J., & Siegel, P. (1996). Understanding the interaction between procedural and distributive justice: The role of trust. In R.M. Kramer & T.R. Tyler (Eds.), *Trust in organizations: Frontiers of theory and research* (pp. 390–413.) Thousand Oaks, CA: Sage; Coutu, D.L. (1998). Organization: Trust in virtual teams. *Harvard Business Review*, 76, 20–21; Crawford, D. (1998, November). A matter of trust. *British Journal of Administrative Management*, 24; Das, T.K., & Teng, B. (1998). Between trust and control: Developing confidence in partner cooperation in alliances.

Academy of Management Review, 23, 491–512. Dwivedi, R.S. (1983). Management by trust: A conceptual model. *Group & Organization Studies, 8*, 375–402; Fukuyama, F. (1995). *Trust: The social virtues and the creation of prosperity.* New York: The Free Press; Gibbs, J., & Gibson, S. (1998). Organizational effectiveness. *Internal Auditor, 55*, 34–36; Ingham, M., & Mothe, C. (1998). How to learn in R&D partnerships. *R & D Management, 28*, 249–261; Jones, T.M., & Bowie, N.E. (1998). Moral hazards on the road to the "virtual" corporation. *Business Ethics Quarterly, 8*, 273–292; Leana, C.R., & Van Buren, H.J. III (1999). Organizational social capital and employment practices. *Academy of Management Review, 24*, 538–555; Maccoby, M. (1998). Making values work. *Research-Technology Management, 41*, 55–57; Meyerson, D., Weick, K.E., & Kramer, R.M. (1996). Swift trust and temporary groups. In R.M. Kramer & T.R. Tyler (Eds.), *Trust in organizations: Frontiers of theory and research* (pp. 261–287). Thousand Oaks, CA: Sage; Miles, R.E., & Snow, C.C. (1995, Summer). Causes of failure in network organizations. *California Management Review*, 72–93; Mishra, A.K. (1996). Organizational responses to crisis: The centrality of trust. In R.M. Kramer & T.R. Tyler (Eds.), *Trust in organizations: Frontiers of theory and research* (pp. 261–287). Thousand Oaks, CA: Sage; Nahapiet, J., & Ghostal, S. (1998). Social capital, intellectual capital and the organization advantage. *Academy of Management Review, 22*, 226–256; Putnam, R. (1993). *Making democracy work.* Princeton, NJ: Princeton University Press; Rousseau, D.M., Sitkin, S.B., Burt, R.S., & Camerer, C. (1998). Not so different after all: Cross-discipline view of trust. *Academy of Management Review, 23*, 393–404; Rule, E., & Keown, S. (1998). Competencies of high-performing strategic alliances. *Strategy and Leadership, 26*, 36–37; Sako, M. (1992). *Prices, quality, and trust: Inter-firm relations in Britain and Japan.* New York: Cambridge University Press; Sapienza, H.J., & Korsgaard, M.A. (1996).

Managing investor relations: The impact of procedural justice in establishing and sustaining investor support. *Academy of Management Journal, 39*, 544–574; Tsai, W., & Ghoshal, S. (1998). Social capital and value creation: The role of intra-firm networks. *Academy of Management Journal, 41*, 464–476; Walker, G., Korgut, B., & Shan, W. (1997). Social capital, structural holes, and the formation of an industry network. *Organizational Science, 8*, 109–125; Webb, E.J. (1996). Trust and crisis. In R.M. Kramer & T.R. Tyler (Eds.), *Trust in organizations: Frontiers of theory and research* (pp. 288–301). Thousand Oaks, CA: Sage.

24. For an extensive discussion of high-performance organizations and trust, see Covey, S.M.R., & Merrill, R.R. (2008). *The speed of trust: The one thing that changes everything.* New York: The Free Press: Covey, M. (2008). Trust is a competency. *Chief Learning Officer, 7*, 54–56. For specific references to trust and bottom-line performance, see R. Kramer & K. Cook (Eds.). (2004). *Trust and distrust in organizations: Dilemmas and approaches.* New York: Russell Sage Foundation.

25. For a more extensive discussion of organizational forms and trust, see Kramer, R.M., & Tyler, T.R. (1996). *Trust in organizations.* Thousand Oaks, CA: Sage.

26. Collins, J., & Porras, J. (2002). *Built to last.* New York: HarperCollins.

Chapter Two

1. Shockley-Zalabak, P., Ellis, K., & Cesaria, R. (2000). *Measuring organizational trust: A diagnostic survey and international indicator.* San Francisco: IABC.

2. For more information about OTI testing and validation results, see Shockley-Zalabak, P., Ellis, K., & Cesaria, R. (2000). *Measuring organizational trust: A diagnostic survey and international indicator.* San Francisco: IABC.

3. Peters, T. (1994). *The pursuit of wow!* (p. 165). New York: Vintage Books.

4. For more information about Southwest's story, see http://www.aboutus.org/Southwest.com; Freiberg, K., & Freiberg, J. (1996). *Nuts! Southwest Airlines' crazy recipe for business and personal success* (p. 288). New York: Broadway Books.

5. Freiberg, K., & Freiberg, J. (1996). *Nuts! Southwest Airlines' crazy recipe for business and personal success* (p. 288). New York: Broadway Books; Herskovitz, J. (2002, June 8–9). Job candidates queue up. *New Zealand Herald*, p. C7.

6. Wow, are they that good? (2002, August 5). *BusinessWeek*, 14. Retrieved August 3, 2008, from http://www.businessweek.com/magazine/content/03_05/b3818085.htm.

7. Bills, J. (personal communication, November 20, 2008). An interview conducted by Michael Hackman; van der Wielen, R.P.J. (personal communication, December 9, 2008). An interview conducted by Michael Hackman.

8. Newspaper executive Mary Jacobus dies at 52. (2009, February 22) *Editor & Publisher*. Retrieved March 1, 2009, from http://www.editorandpublisher.com/eandp/news/article_display.jsp?vnu_content_id=1003943608.

9. Jacobus, M. (personal communication, January 26, 2009). An interview conducted by Michael Hackman.

10. 100 best companies to work for. (2008, February 4). *Fortune*. Retrieved August 3, 2008, from http://money.cnn.com/magazines/fortune/bestcompanies/2008/benefits/work_life.html; Top companies for work/life balance. (2008, July 29). *The Glass Hammer*. Retrieved August 3, 2008, from http://www.theglasshammer.com/news/2008/07/29/top-companies-for-worklife-balance/; MITRE named to *Fortune*'s "100 best companies to work for" list for seventh consecutive. . . . (2008, January 24). *Reuters*. Retrieved August 3, 2008, from http://www.reuters.com/article/pressRelease/idUS242741+24-Jan-2008+BW20080124; REI named to *Fortune*'s best places

to work list for eleventh consecutive year. (2008, January 22). *Reuters*. Retrieved August 3, 2008, from http://www .reuters.com/article/pressRelease/idUS215463+22-Jan-2008+BW20080122

11. Albright, B. (personal communication, January 15, 2009). Correspondence with Michael Hackman.

12. Chouinard, Y. (2005). *Let my people go surfing*. New York: Penguin Press.

13. Christopher, W. (2007). *Sustainability case study: Patagonia*. SustainQuest. Retrieved August 1, 2008, from http://sustainquest. com/content/view/23/30/

14. Janega, P. (personal communication, October 14, 2008). An interview conducted by Sherry Morreale at the SIETAR Conference, Granada, Spain.

15. Avram, E. (personal communication, December 15, 2008). These examples were provided to Pam Shockley-Zalabak electronically from Nigeria and Israel.

16. Avram, E. (personal communication, December 15, 2008). These examples were provided electronically from Romania, Bulgaria, Macedonia, and Spain.

Chapter Three

1. Kotter, J.P. (1990). *A force for change: How leadership differs from management* (p. 36). New York: The Free Press.

2. Green, H. (2009, March 2). How Amazon aims to keep clicking. *BusinessWeek*, pp. 34–40; McGregor, J. (2008, March 3). Customer service champs. *BusinessWeek*, p. 37; McGregor, J. (2008, March 3). The 2008 winners. *BusinessWeek*, pp. 47–52.

3. For information on the vision statements listed and vision in general, see Abrahams, J. (1995). *The mission statement book*. Berkeley, CA: Ten Speed Press; Collins, J.C., & Porras, J.I. (1996, September/October). Building your company's

vision. *Harvard Business Review*, pp. 65–77; Disney Institute. (2001). *Be our guest*. New York: Disney Enterprises; Hughes, R.L., & Beatty, K.C. (2005). *Becoming a strategic leader*. San Francisco: Jossey-Bass; Zaccaro, S.J., & Banks, D.J. (2001). Leadership, vision, and organizational effectiveness. In S.J. Zaccaro & R.K. Klimoski (Eds.), *The nature of organizational leadership* (pp. 181–218). San Francisco: Jossey-Bass.

4. Rewers, A. (personal communication, January 14, 2009). Correspondence with Michael Hackman.

5. Hesselbein, F. (personal communication, November, 2008). A discussion and presentation at the International Leadership Association in Los Angeles, CA; For an extensive discussion of her view, see Hesselbein, F. (2002). *Hesselbein on leadership*. San Francisco: Jossey-Bass.

6. Bills, J. (personal communication, November 20, 2008). An interview conducted by Michael Hackman.

7. van der Wielen, R.P.J. (personal communication, December 9, 2008). Electronic correspondence with Michael Hackman.

8. Friedman, T. (2006). *The world is flat: A brief history of the twenty-first century*. New York: Farrar, Straus & Giroux.

9. Dobbin, B. (2005, September 9). Digital camera turns 30—sort of. MSNBC.com. Retrieved August 10, 2008, from http://www.msnbc.msn.com/id/9261340/; Otsuki, T. (2008, February 20). Samsung Techwin takes 3rd place in digital camera market share Tech-on. Retrieved August 20, 2008, from http://techon.nikkeibp.co.jp/english/NEWS_EN/20080220/147706/

10. Stark, P. (personal communication, October 22, 2008). An interview conducted by Sherry Morreale at the SIETAR Conference, Granada, Spain.

11. For more information about stakeholders' distrust of competence, see Connell, J., & Ferres, N. (2003). Engendering trust in manager-subordinate relationships. *Personnel Review, 32*, 560–587; Cunningham, J.B., & MacGregor, J. (2000). Trust and the design of work: Complementary constructs

in satisfaction and performance. *Human Relations, 53,* 1575–1591; Mullen, B., & Copper, C. (1994). The relation between group cohesiveness and performance: An integration. *Psychological Bulletin, 115,* 210–227; Brown, H.G., Poole, M.S., & Rodgers, T.L. (2004). Interpersonal traits, complementarity, and trust in virtual collaboration. *Journal of Management Information Systems, 20,* 115–137; Ciancutti, A., & Steding, T. (2000). *Built on trust: Gaining competitive advantage in any organization.* Chicago: Contemporary Books.

12. Emirates cancels orders for 20 Airbus jets. (2006, October 30). MSNBC.com. Retrieved August 4, 2008, from http://www.msnbc.msn.com; FedEx cancels Airbus aircraft order. (2006), November 7). MSNBC.com. Retrieved August 4, 2008, from http://www.msnbc.msn.com.

13. Matlack, C. (2006, October 23). Wayward Airbus. *BusinessWeek,* pp. 46–48.

14. Quinn, L., Kuman R., & Avram, E. (personal communication, December, 2008). Personal interviews and electronic communication with Pam Shockley-Zalabak; Rewers, A. (personal communication, January 14, 2009). Correspondence with Michael Hackman.

15. Capodagli, B., & Jackson, L. (1999). *The Disney way* (p. 87). New York: McGraw-Hill.

16. For more information, see Collins, J. (2001). *Good to great.* New York: HarperCollins.

17. McQueen, R. (1998). *The Eaton's: The rise and fall of Canada's royal family.* Toronto: Stoddard (Sharpe and Korthals quotes on p. 285); Poulin, B.J., & Hackman, M.Z. (2001). The rise and fall of the T. Eaton Company of Canada: Lasting lessons on leadership and strategy. *The Journal of Leadership Studies, 8,* 96–112; Poulin, B.J., Hackman, M.Z., & Barbarasa-Mihai, C. (2007). Leadership and succession: The challenge to succeed and the vortex of failure. *Leadership, 3,* 301–324.

18. Holzman, D. (1993, August). When workers run the show. *Working Woman*, pp. 38–41, 72–74; Managing the journey (1990, November). *Inc.*, pp. 45–54; Peters, T. (1992). *Liberation management* (pp. 238–243). New York: Ballantine; Pomeroy, A. (2004, July). Great places, inspired employees. *HR Magazine*; Stayer, R. (1990, November/December). How I learned to let my workers lead. *Harvard Business Review*, pp. 66–83.

19. Marchionne, B. (2008, December). Fiat's extreme makeover. *Harvard Business Review*, pp. 45–48.

20. Cesaria, R. (personal communication, March 2009). Electronic correspondence with Pam Shockley-Zalabak.

21. Marchionne, S. (2008, December). Fiat's extreme makeover. *Harvard Business Review*, pp. 45–48.

Chapter Four

1. For an extensive discussion of Roosevelt and Stalin, see Sample, S.B. (2003). *The contrarian's guide to leadership*. San Francisco: Jossey-Bass.

2. For a comprehensive biography of Truman, see McCullough, D. (1992). *Truman*. New York: Simon and Schuster.

3. For more information and a review of research on communication and trust, see Shockley-Zalabak, P. (2009). *Fundamentals of organizational communication* (7th ed.). Boston: Allyn & Bacon.

4. Wagner, M. (2009, February 26). Shareholders criticize Apple over Jobs' health disclosures. *The Information Week* blog. Retrieved March 1, 2003, from http://www.informationweek.com/blog/main/archives/2009/02/shareholders_cr.html.

5. *Fortune* magazine names Bear Stearns "most admired" securities firm. *Business Wire*. (2005, February 25). Retrieved February 11, 2009, from http://findarticles.com/p/articles/mi_m0EIN/is_2005_Feb_25/ai_n10302819

6. Boyd, R. (2008, March 31). The last days of Bear Stearns. *Fortune*. Retrieved February 11, 2009, from http://money .cnn.com/2008/03/28/magazines/fortune/boyd_bear.fortune/

7. Boyd, R. (2008, March 31).

8. Burrough, B. (2008, August). Bringing down Bear Stearns. *Vanity Fair*. Retrieved February 11, 2009, from http://www .vanityfair.com/politics/features/2008/08/bear_stearns200808 ?currentPage=1.

9. Boyd, R. (2008, March 31).

10. Kelly, K. (2009). *Street fighters: The last 72 hours of Bear Stearns, the toughest firm on Wall Street* (p. 225). New York: Portfolio.

11. Texas orders recall of all products ever shipped from peanut plant amid salmonella outbreak. (2009, February 11). *The Atlanta Journal-Constitution*.

12. Nation's peanut growers reeling from outbreak. Retrieved February 16, 2009, from http://www.msnbc.msn.com/ id292120000/

13. For more information about distortions in communication, see Shockley-Zalabak, P. (2009). *Fundamentals of organizational communication* (7th ed.). Boston: Allyn & Bacon.

14. For more information about barriers to change, see Shockley-Zalabak, P. (2009). *Fundamentals of organizational communication* (7th ed.). Boston: Allyn & Bacon.

15. United States Intelligence Community Information Sharing Strategy. (2008, February 22). Washington, DC: Office of the Director of National Intelligence, Director of National Intelligence.

16. Holtz, S. (2009, March 11). "Social Media Boot Camp." Presentation at the Social Media for Communicators Conference, Las Vegas, Nevada, reported by Michael Hackman.

17. Holtz, S. (2009, March 11).

18. Edelman, R. (2009). *Edelman Trust Barometer executive summary.* Retrieved March 16, 2009, from http://www.scribd.com/doc/11484809/Edelman-Trust-Barometer-2009-Summary.
19. Holtz, S. (2009, March 11).
20. Holtz, S. (2009, March 11).
21. For an extensive discussion of leadership communication, see Sample, S.B. (2003). *The contrarian's guide to leadership.* San Francisco: Jossey-Bass.
22. Rewers, A. (personal communication, January 14, 2009). Correspondence with Michael Hackman.
23. The authentic enterprise. (2007). The Arthur W. Page Society page. Retrieved September 17, 2009, from http://www:awpagesociety.com/images/uploads/2007Authentic Enterprise.pdf.
24. Secrets of top performers: How companies with highly effective employee communication differentiate themselves. (2007/2008). Watson Wyatt ROI Study.
25. Meyerrose, D. (personal communication, October 13, 2008). An interview conducted by Pam Shockley-Zalabak and electronic communication.
26. Meyerrose, D. (2008, October 13).

Chapter Five

1. Skorman, R., & Seator, P. (personal communication, January 30, 2009). An interview conducted by Sherry Morreale.
2. For more information about Covey's concepts, see Covey, S.M.R. (2001). *The speed of trust: The one thing that changes everything.* New York: The Free Press.
3. For an extensive discussion of how employees have lost faith in those at the top, see Branham, L. (2005). *The 7 hidden reasons employees leave: How to recognize the subtle signs before it's too late.* New York: American Management Association; Branham, L. (2001). *Keeping the people who*

keep you in business: 24 ways to hang on to your most valu-able talent. New York: American Management Association; Stafford, D. (2008, April 6). Leaders key to workers leaving. *Gazette.* Retrieved August 15, 2008, from http://www.gazette.com

4. For more information about CEO compensation, see Hackman, M.Z., & Johnson, C.E. (2009). *Leadership: A communication perspective* (5th ed.). Long Grove, IL: Waveland.

5. Landry, H. (2008, November 24–30). Executive pay sparks outrage. *Washington Post National Weekly Edition*, pp. 7–8.

6. CEO compensation not well related to companies' stock returns: Study. *Canadian Press Newswire.* Retrieved January 22, 2007, from LexisNexis Academic.

7. Lublin, J.S. (2006, October 12). Executive pay soars despite attempted restraints. *Associated Press Financial Wire.* Retrieved January 22, 2007, from LexisNexis Academic; Grow, B., Foust, D., Thornton, E., Farzad, R., McGregor, J., Zegle, S., & Javers, E. (2007, January 15). Out at Home Depot. *BusinessWeek*, pp. 56–62. Retrieved January 22, 2007, from Ebsco Host.

8. Landry. (2008, November 24–30).

9. Coca-Cola's secret formula is not for sale. (2006, July 6). WBZ-TV. Retrieved February 11, 2009, from http://wbztv.com/video/?id=21974@wbz.dayport.com.

10. Pepsi alerted Coca-Cola to stolen-Coke-secrets offer. (2006, July 6). FoxNews.com. Retrieved February 11, 2009, from http://www.foxnews.com/story/0,2933,202439,00.html.

11. For more information about developing communication to support trust, see Lee, G. (2006). *Courage: The backbone of leadership.* San Francisco: Jossey-Bass.

12. *Fortune* ranks CH2M HILL one of "100 Best Companies to Work For." Retrieved February 12, 2009, from http://www.msnbc.msn.com/id/28858494/

13. Woodbury, D. (2009, February 4). CH2M HILL runs against the tide. *Rocky Mountain News*, p. B3.

14. *Fortune* ranks CH2M HILL one of "100 Best Companies to Work For." Retrieved February 12, 2009, from http://www .msnbc.msn.com/id/28858494/
15. Howland, J. (1982). Copyright © CH2M HILL.

Chapter Six

1. Drummond, J. (personal communication, December 2008). An interview conducted by Pam Shockley-Zalabak with the founder and chairman of the board, Jim Drummond (not his real name), who desires to remain anonymous.
2. Although we have permission to use this example, the names and some circumstances have been changed based on the nature of the example.
3. Graham, J.L., & Lam, N.M. (2004). The Chinese negotiation. In *On doing business in China* (pp. 31–55). Boston, MA: Harvard Business School Press, p. 33.
4. Graham & Lam, p. 40.
5. Graham & Lam, pp. 43, 53–54.
6. Ahrens, F. (2009, February 9). McDonald's sales continue surge. Washington.Post.com. http://voices.washingtonpost. com/economy-watch/2009/02/mcdonalds_sales_continue_ surge.html; Arndt, M. (2007, February 5). McDonald's 24/7. *BusinessWeek*, pp. 64–72; Belasen, A.T. (2008). *The theory and practice of corporate communication*. Thousand Oaks, CA: Sage; Cowan, J. (2002, November). Is McDonald's really so bad? *enRoute*, pp. 79–84; Daniels, J.L., & Daniels, N.C. (1993). *Global vision*. New York: McGraw-Hill; Happy meal. (2007, January 27). *The Economist*, pp. 64–65; What's this? The French love McDonald's? (2003, January 13). *BusinessWeek*, p. 50.
7. Customer service champs (2009, March 2). *BusinessWeek*, pp. 32–33. Retrieved March 2, 2009, from www.usaa.com.
8. McGregor, J. (2007, December 19). Employee innovator: USAA. *Fast Company*. Retrieved March 8, 2009, from

http://www.fastcompany.com/magazine/99/open_customer-usaa.html.

9. Andrews, V. (personal communication, March 6, 2009). An interview with Michael Hackman.

Chapter Seven

1. Sanders, B. (1995). *Fabled service* (p. 75). San Francisco: Jossey-Bass.

2. Spector, R. (2001). *Lessons from the Nordstrom way* (p. 68). Hoboken, NJ: John Wiley & Sons.

3. For more information about benefits and incentives, see Robert Spector's website at: http://www.robertspector.com/index.cfm.

4. For an extensive discussion of organizational identification, values, culture, and organizational effectiveness, see Shockley-Zalabak, P., & Morley, D. (1989). Adhering to organizational culture: What does it mean? Why does it matter? *Group & Organization Studies,14*, 483–500; Morley, D., & Shockley-Zalabak, P. (1991). Setting the rules: An examination of the influence of organizational founders' values. *Management Communication Quarterly, 4*, 422–449; and Shockley-Zalabak, P., & Morley, D. (1994). Creating a culture: A longitudinal examination of the influence of management and employee values on communication rule stability and emergence. *Human Communication Research, 20*, 334–355.

5. For a full discussion of the Collins and Porras research, see Collins, J., & Porras, J. (2002). *Built to last: Successful habits of visionary companies*. New York: HarperCollins.

6. For more information and research supporting the Hui and Lee perspective, see Hui, C., & Lee, C. (2000). Moderating effects of organization-based self-esteem on organizational uncertainty: Employee response relationships. *Journal of Management, 26*, 215–232.

7. For more information and the results of research supporting this claim, see Shockley-Zalabak, P., Ellis, K., & Cesaria, R. (2000). *Measuring organizational trust: A diagnostic survey and international indicator*. San Francisco: International Association of Business Communicators.

8. For a discussion of the relationship between trust and antisocial work behaviors, see Thau, S., Crossley, C., Bennett, R.J., & Sezesny, S. (2007). The relationship between trust, attachment, and antisocial work behaviors. *Human Relations*, 60, 1155–1179.

9. For more information about Zappos' culture, see *Zappos 2008 culture book*. (2008). Zappos, Inc.

10. Hsieh, T. (2009, March 12). "Tapping into the power of social media to build a brand that inspires employees and draws in customers." A presentation at the Social Media for Communicators Conference, Las Vegas, Nevada.

11. Lacy, S. (2009, July 22). Amazon buys Zappos: The price is $928m., not $847m. Retrieved September 20, 2009, from http://www.techcrunch.com/2009/07/22/amazon-buys-zappos/

12. Bartholomew, M. (personal communication, October 23, 2008). An interview conducted by Sherry Morreale at the SIETAR Conference, Granada, Spain.

13. For more information and the research supporting these claims, see Hui, C., & Lee, C. (2000). Moderating effects of organization-based self-esteem on organizational uncertainty: Employee response relationships. *Journal of Management*, 26, 215–232; and Thau, S., Crossley, C., Bennett, R.J., & Sezesny, S. (2007). The relationship between trust, attachment, and antisocial work behaviors. *Human Relations*, 60, 1155–1179.

14. Sorry, don't know anyone by that name. (2009, March 9). *BusinessWeek*, p. 9.

15. For a discussion of leader communication skills and practices to support loyalty, see Mayfield, J., & Mayfield, M. (2002, June). Leader communication strategies: Critical paths

to improving employee commitment. *American Business Review*, pp. 89–94; Robbins, S. (2001). *Organizational behavior: Concepts, controversies, applications*. Englewood Cliffs, NJ: Prentice Hall; and Young, M., & Post, J.E. (1993, Summer). Managing to communicate, communicating to manage. *Organizational Dynamics*, pp. 31–43.

16. For an extensive discussion of framing, see Fairhurst, G., & Sarr, R. (1996). *The art of framing: Managing the language of leadership*. San Francisco: Jossey-Bass.

17. Gabel, P. (personal communication, October 2008). A telephone interview with Sherry Morreale and Ruggero Cesaria.

Chapter Eight

1. For a discussion of rapid change and new organizational forms, see Shockley-Zalabak, P. (2002). Protean places: Teams across time and space. *Journal of Applied Communication Research, 30*, 231–250.

2. For more information about trust in global organizations, see Handy, C. (1995, May/June). Trust and the virtual organization. *Harvard Business Review*, pp. 40–50.

3. For an extensive discussion of the changing global environment, see Friedman, T. (2006). *The world is flat*. New York: Faraar, Straus and Giroux.

4. For a comprehensive discussion of the importance of differences in cultural perspectives, see Caldwell, C., & Clapham, S. (2003). Organizational trustworthiness: An international perspective. *Journal of Business Ethics, 47*, 349–364; Hofstede, G. (1995). *Cultures and organizations: Software of the mind*. New York: McGraw-Hill; and Hofstede, G. (2001). *Culture's consequences: Comparing values, behaviors, institutions and organizations across nations*. Thousand Oaks, CA: Sage.

5. Lake, R.A. (personal communication, October 23, 2008). An interview with Sherry Morreale at the SIETAR Conference, Granada, Spain.

6. Researchers in the SIETAR Italia study of cultural differences in trust include David Trickey, project coordinator and questionnaire developer; Marianna Amy Crestani, project support coordinator and presenter; Ruth Ann Lake and Patti Janega, workshop developers; and Elio Vera and Goffredo Diana, project supporters.

7. For more information and research on contextual confidence and trust development, see Child, J., & Mollering, G. (2003). Contextual confidence and active trust development in the Chinese business environment. *Organization Science, 14*, 69–80.

8. For a discussion of institution-based trustworthiness in international and electronic contexts, see Caldwell, C., & Clapham, S. (2003). Organizational trustworthiness: An international perspective. *Journal of Business Ethics, 47*, 349–364; and Pavlou, P. (2002). Institution-based trust in interorganizational exchange relationships: The role of online B2B marketplaces on trust formation. *Journal of Strategic Information Systems, 11*, 215–243.

9. For a discussion of trust in virtual organizations, see Handy, C. (1995, May/June). Trust and the virtual organization. *Harvard Business Review*, pp. 40–50.

10. For an extensive discussion of the concept of "good to great," see Collins, J. (2001). *Good to great*. New York: HarperCollins.

11. For more information about innovation and 3M, see Conceiao, P., Hamill, D., & Pinheiro, P. (2002). Innovative science and technology commercialization strategies at 3M: A case study. *Journal of Engineering and Technology Management, 19*, 25–38; Dubashi, J. (1992, February 18). 3M: New talent and products outweigh the costs. *Financial World, 19*; Hindo, B. (2007, June 11). At 3M, a struggle between efficiency and creativity. *BusinessWeek*, pp. 8–14; Katauskas, T. (1990, November). Follow-through: 3M's formula for success. *Research and Development*, pp. 46–52; Lehr, L.W. (1988). Encouraging innovation and entrepreneurship in diversified

corporations. In R.L. Kuhn (Ed.), *Handbook for creative and innovative managers* (pp. 211–229). New York: McGraw-Hill; Mitchell, R. (1989, April 10). Masters of innovation: How 3M keeps its new products coming. *BusinessWeek*, pp. 58–63; Mitchell, R. (1989, Innovation Issue). Mining the work force for ideas. *BusinessWeek*, p. 121; Mitsch, R.A. (1992, September/October). R&D at 3M: Continuing to play a big role. *Research Technology Management*, pp. 22–26; Zand, D.E. (1997). *The leadership triad: Knowledge, trust, and power*. New York: Oxford University Press.

12. Jacobus, M. (personal communication, January 26, 2009). An interview with Michael Hackman.

13. For an extensive discussion of strategy models, see Lewis, L., Hamel, S., & Richardson, B. (2001). Communicating change to nonprofit stakeholders. *Management Communication Quarterly, 15*, 5–41.

14. For more information and research relating trust and leadership conflict and trust during conflict between managers and employees, see Korsgaard, M.A., Brodt, S., & Whitener, E. (2002). Trust in the face of conflict: The role of managerial trustworthy behavior and organizational context. *Journal of Applied Psychology, 87*, 312–319; and Simons, T., & Peterson, R. (2000). Task conflict and relationship conflict in top management teams: The pivotal role of intragroup trust. *Journal of Applied Psychology, 85*, 102–111.

15. For an extensive discussion of public reaction to crises, see Stocker, K. (1997). A strategic approach to crisis management. In C.L. Caywood (Ed.), *Handbook of strategic public relations and integrated communications*. New York: McGraw-Hill.

16. For more information and references for developing a crisis plan, see Shockley-Zalabak, P. (2009). *Fundamentals of organizational communication* (7th ed.) Boston: Allyn & Bacon.

17. For the report of best practices for crisis communication, see Seeger, M. (2006). Best practices in crisis communication:

An expert panel process. *Journal of Applied Communication Research, 34,* 232–244.

18. Gomez, R. (personal communication, November 11, 2008). A telephone interview with Sherry Morreale.

19. For an extensive discussion of the research supporting these arguments, see Shockley-Zalabak, P. (2009). *Fundamentals of organizational communication* (7th ed.) Boston: Allyn & Bacon.

20. Rewers, A. (personal communication, January 14, 2009). Correspondence with Michael Hackman.

Chapter Nine

1. For an extensive discussion of the impact of downsizing on trust, see Tourish, D., Paulsen, N., Hobman, E., & Bordia, P. (2004). The downsides of downsizing: Communication processes and information needs in the aftermath of a workforce reduction strategy. *Management Communication Quarterly, 17,* 485–516.

Acknowledgements

Writing a book with three authors is a wonderfully collaborative activity. However, more than the three of us have made this journey possible. We want to acknowledge the important work of Kathy Ellis and Ruggero Cesaria in the development of the Organizational Trust Index (OTI), funded by a grant from the International Association of Business Communicators Research Foundation under the guidance of Natasha Nicholson. In developing the OTI, we were assisted in our global data collection efforts by Gaynelle Winograd and Charles Zalabak. For this book, three long-time colleagues, Ruggero Cesaria, Eugen Avram, and Marianna Crestani, provided invaluable assistance in interviewing individuals in countries throughout Europe, Asia, and the Mid-East. We would not have the rich global perspectives on trust this book provides without their efforts. We, of course, want to acknowledge our many clients who agreed to be a part of the examples in this book and all those who graciously agreed to our interview requests. A special thanks goes to Jeff Rath, who as a graduate student served as our research assistant, and to Carmen Stavrositu, who provided data analysis along with our Italian colleagues. Finally, our deepest thanks go to our families, who have provided and continue to provide the ongoing love and support that makes all things possible— to Charles Zalabak, Jim and Leatha Shockley, Yvonne Zalabak Cotter, Carissa Cotter, Samantha Klingenberg, Jesse Morreale, Zak and Vanden Klingenberg, Jane Hackman, Zachary Hackman, and Aubrey Hackman.

About the Authors

Dr. Pamela S. Shockley-Zalabak is chancellor and a professor of communication at the University of Colorado at Colorado Springs. The author of seven books and over one hundred articles and productions on organizational communication, Dr. Shockley-Zalabak's research interests include organizational trust and cultures as they relate to overall organizational effectiveness. Prior to assuming her chancellor responsibilities, Dr. Shockley-Zalabak was vice chancellor for student success and the founding chair of the UCCS Communication Department. Dr. Shockley-Zalabak's books include *Fundamentals of Organizational Communication: Knowledge, Sensitivity, Skills, and Values; Understanding Organizational Communication: Commentaries, Cases, and Conversations; The Power of Networked Teams: Hewlett-Packard's Colorado Springs Story; Case Studies for Organizational Communication: Understanding Communication Processes; and Engaging Communication, Transforming Organizations: Scholarship of Engagement in Action*. Dr. Shockley-Zalabak also is president of CommuniCon, Inc., a consulting organization working with clients in the United States, Europe, and Asia, and is the producer of award-winning television documentaries aired nationally and in major U.S. markets.

Dr. Sherwyn P. Morreale is a faculty member in the Department of Communication at the University of Colorado at Colorado Springs. She also serves as director of graduate studies in communication and directs the department's assessment activities for the graduate program. Dr. Morreale's main research and teaching interests include organizational communication, communication theory, business and professional communication, instructional communication, public speaking, and the assessment of communication competence. Her research has appeared in the *Basic Communication Course Annual, Communication Education, The Communicator, Education,* the *Journal of the Association for Communication Administration,* and *The Successful Professor.* She is the lead author of two communication textbooks and has authored numerous articles and chapters for collected volumes and special monographs in the communication discipline. Recently, she penned two entries for national and international encyclopedias on the nature of communication competence and a new volume entitled *Getting the Most from Your Graduate Education in Communication: A Student's Handbook,* published by the National Communication Association (NCA) and distributed to every graduate program in the country.

From 1997 to 2006, Dr. Morreale served as the associate director of NCA, the oldest and largest association of professors in the communication discipline in the world. In her position at NCA, she was responsible for communication instruction and research initiatives and outreach on behalf of the communication discipline to funding agencies, policy makers, and other private and public audiences. Prior to 1997, she taught in the Communication Department at the University of Colorado at Colorado Springs and directed the activities of the Center for Excellence in Oral Communication on the campus.

Dr. Michael Z. Hackman is a professor in the Department of Communication and the director of the Honors Program at the University of Colorado at Colorado Springs. He also serves as an Adjunct at the Center for Creative Leadership and an affiliate with the consulting firms CommuniCon, Inc., Executive Forum, Footprints Consulting, and the TRACOM Group. Dr. Hackman teaches courses in communication and leadership at both the undergraduate and graduate levels, including courses that were supported by a grant from the U.S. Department of Education Fund for the Improvement of Post-Secondary Education (FIPSE) that allowed for the development of an online curriculum in organizational communication and leadership delivered to students and working professionals in the United States and Europe. In 1995, he was awarded the university-wide Outstanding Teacher Award.

Dr. Hackman's research focuses on a wide range of issues, including the impact of gender and culture on communication and leadership behavior, leadership succession, organizational trust, instructional communication in mediated contexts, and creativity. His work has appeared in such journals as *Communication Education*, *Communication Quarterly*, *Distance Education*, *The Journal of Leadership Studies*, *Leadership*, *The Leadership Review*, *Perceptual and Motor Skills*, and the *Southern Speech Communication Journal*. He is also the co-author (with Craig Johnson) of two books, *Leadership: A Communication Perspective* and *Creative Communication: Principles and Applications*.

Dr. Hackman has extensive experience as a consultant. He has developed and delivered training, guided organizational development initiatives, and provided executive coaching services for more than two hundred public and private sector organizations throughout the United States and in Australia, Austria, Canada, China, Italy, Luxembourg, the Netherlands, and New Zealand. His clients have included Agilent Technologies, Bristol-Myers Squibb, Ernst & Young, Fiat, Georgia-Pacific, Harley-Davidson, Hewlett-Packard, Kimberly-Clark, NASA, Medtronic, Philips, Telecom New Zealand, the United States Air Force, the United States Golf Association, URL Pharma, and Wells Fargo.

Index

Page references followed by *fig* indicate an illustrated figure; followed by *t* indicate an table.

About the International Association of Business Communicators

The International Association of Business Communicators (IABC) is a global network of over thirteen thousand communication professionals in sixty-seven countries, one hundred chapters, and ten thousand organizations. Established in 1970, IABC ensures that its members have the skills and resources to progress in their careers, develop and share best practices, set standards of excellence, build credibility and respect for the profession, and unite as a community. IABC members practice the disciplines of corporate communication, public relations, employee communication, marketing communication, media relations, community relations, public affairs, investor relations, and government relations.

Programs

IABC sponsors several conferences throughout the year in addition to its annual international conference. To further the education of communication professionals, IABC offers monthly teleseminars and web seminars. IABC honors the best in the profession with the Gold Quill Awards program and the accreditation program. IABC also maintains an online job board.

Publications

The publishing division of IABC offers books, manuals, and communication templates on a number of organizational communication topics. IABC also publishes the award-winning, bimonthly magazine, *Communication World*, and a monthly online newsletter, *CW Bulletin*.

Research

The IABC Research Foundation is a nonprofit corporation dedicated to the support and advancement of organizational communication by delivering research findings vital to the profession. The Foundation translates leading-edge communication theory into real-world practice, helping communicators be effective and visionary in their work. Founded in 1970, the Foundation is building a research portfolio aligned with a new research agenda. The Foundation offers grants for communication research in support of this agenda. Learn more about the International Association of Business Communicators at www .iabc.com.

Pres.
Provost > tell us about you are good at; tell us
who is doing the rest

What makes you feel like the university
cares for you?